中国—东盟博览会蓝皮书

中国—东盟经贸合作展望报告

2024—2025

Vision on China–ASEAN Economic and Trade Cooperation

中国—东盟博览会秘书处
China-ASEAN Expo Secretariat

广西大学中国—东盟经济学院
China-ASEAN School of Economics, Guangxi University

编 著

中国商务出版社

·北京·

图书在版编目（CIP）数据

中国—东盟经贸合作展望报告 = Vision on China-ASEAN Economic and Trade Cooperation. 2024—2025：汉英对照 / 中国-东盟博览会秘书处，广西大学中国-东盟经济学院编著. -- 北京：中国商务出版社，2024.9.

ISBN 978-7-5103-5324-6

Ⅰ. F752.733

中国国家版本馆 CIP 数据核字第 2024UK9652 号

中国—东盟经贸合作展望报告 2024—2025

Vision on China-ASEAN Economic and Trade Cooperation 2024—2025

中国—东盟博览会秘书处　广西大学中国—东盟经济学院　编著

出版发行：中国商务出版社有限公司

地　　址：北京市东城区安定门外大街东后巷 28 号　　　邮　　编：100710

网　　址：http://www.cctpress.com

联系电话：010—64515150（发行部）　　010—64212247（总编室）
　　　　　010—64243656（事业部）　　010—64248236（印制部）

责任编辑：李自满

排　　版：北京天逸合文化有限公司

印　　刷：宝蕾元仁浩（天津）印刷有限公司

开　　本：710 毫米×1000 毫米　1/16

印　　张：13.75　　　　　　　　字　　数：156 千字

版　　次：2024 年 9 月第 1 版　　　印　　次：2024 年 9 月第 1 次印刷

书　　号：ISBN 978-7-5103-5324-6

定　　价：88.00 元

编 委 会

写在前面的话（代序）

中国与东盟国家山水相连，人文相亲，友好交往源远流长。双方从 1991 年建立对话关系，2003 年建立战略伙伴关系，到 2021 年提升为全面战略伙伴关系，实现了跨越式发展，成为亚太区域合作中最为成功和最具活力的典范，成为推动构建人类命运共同体的生动例证。

由中国和东盟 10 国经贸主管部门及东盟秘书处共同主办、广西壮族自治区承办的中国—东盟博览会（东博会）已走过 20 年历程，与中国—东盟友好关系相伴相随，与中国—东盟自由贸易区（以下简称中国—东盟自贸区）共同成长，成为中国—东盟重要的开放平台、中国—东盟自贸区建设的助推器、中国—东盟合作的"南宁渠道"、推进区域经济一体化的务实平台、广西亮丽的名片，为服务构建更为紧密的中国—东盟命运共同体发挥了重要作用。

贸易与投资是中国—东盟合作的重要内容，促进中国—东盟经贸合作是东博会的初心和使命。20 年来，东博会平台汇聚了中国和东盟国家的企业、商品、服务、项目、资金、信息等海量资源，持续为双方企业相互开拓市场创造商机，助力双方互为最大贸易伙伴和相互投资最活跃的合作伙伴，推动一大批重大机制和项目落地，促进中国—东盟自贸区从 1.0 版到 2.0 版并升级到 3.0 版。

当前，百年未有之大变局加速演进，世界经济复苏缓慢，国际市场需求不振，经济全球化遭遇逆流，单边主义、保护主义明显上升。在新形势下，东博会开启"镶钻成冠"升级发展新征程，持续完善平台功能，更好促进中国—东盟区域经济增长，为构建开放型世界经济作出更大贡献。为强化东博会经贸合作促进平台功能，支持实体经济高质量发展，东博会秘书处与广西大学合作出版东博会蓝皮书——《中国—东盟经贸合作展望报告》，从2024年起每年在东博会会期发布。本书具有以下特点：

一是权威性。本书信息主要来源于中国和东盟有关政府部门，并由知名智库和业界专家进行解读分析和趋势预判，为企业界和学界提供有公信力的观点和信息支持。

二是前瞻性。本书不仅对上年度以来中国—东盟经贸合作进行回顾分析，对亮点、重点、特点、难点进行评述，而且对下年度双方经贸合作进行趋势展望，提出的观点具有前瞻意义，丰富了各方对趋势展望进行思考和预判的维度。

三是实用性。本书创新提出中国—东盟经贸合作的明星行业、明星企业、明星产品、合作新业态等，内容翔实，数据丰富，案例典型，针对性强，适合从事中国—东盟经贸合作的企业和研究人员阅读，对实际工作具有决策参考作用。

本报告是中国—东盟博览会秘书处，广西大学中国—东盟经济研究院、中国—东盟研究院等各位专家共同努力下完成的，欢迎指正。

目　录
CONTENTS

综　述

中国和东盟是互利共赢的好伙伴。中国—东盟经贸合作作为双方关系发展的重要支柱，在促进地区经济增长、构建更为紧密的中国—东盟命运共同体中发挥着重要作用。2023 年以来，在中国和东盟领导人的战略引领下，中国与东盟落实中国—东盟自贸区各项协定，双边经贸合作持续增长，呈现出强劲韧性和活力。展望 2025 年，双方经贸合作将有望延续快速发展势头。

一、2023 年以来中国—东盟经贸合作回顾

2023 年，中国和东盟货物贸易、投资合作、服务贸易取得新成效，中国—东盟自贸区 3.0 版谈判取得了新进展。

一是货物贸易保持高位。2023 年双边贸易规模达 9117 亿美元。2024 年上半年，双边贸易额达 4724.5 亿美元，同比增长 7.1%，增速在中国主要贸易伙伴中位居第一，双方继续互为最大贸易合作伙伴。

二是相互投资强劲增长。截至 2023 年底，中国和东盟累计相互投资额超过 3800 亿美元。2024 年上半年，中国对东盟直接投资 107.5 亿美元，同比增长 74%；东盟对华直接投资 64.6 亿美元，同比增长 12.9%。中国和东盟保持相互投资最活跃的合作伙伴。

三是服务贸易加速扩张。旅游合作方面，在互免旅游签证政策加

持下，双方直航航班数达到每周 2300 多班，双方旅游者互访人数迅速恢复，如 2023 年泰国共接待中国游客 350 万人次，2024 年一季度超过 175 万人次，中国在各国游客数量中位居第一。同时，越南、马来西亚、泰国、菲律宾、新加坡跻身 2023 年度中国入境旅游十大客源地国家（地区）。金融合作方面，中国—东盟双边本币互换协议金额超 8000 亿元，东盟地区人民币跨境清算网络初具规模。电子商务合作方面，中国—东盟电子商务合作发展指数首次发布，拼多多等电商平台纷纷入驻东盟国家。

四是中国—东盟自贸区 3.0 版谈判加快推进。2023 年启动首轮谈判以来，双方围绕数字经济、绿色经济、货物贸易、投资、经济技术合作、卫生与植物卫生措施等多个领域深入交换意见，推动在现有中国—东盟自贸协定基础上，进一步提升贸易投资自由化水平，拓展新兴领域务实合作，打造更高水平中国—东盟自贸区。2024 年 6 月，第 7 轮谈判在广西南宁举行，双方在原有基础上，实质性完成竞争和消费者保护、供应链互联互通、标准技术法规与合格评定程序等章节谈判。

二、2023 年以来中国—东盟经贸合作评析

纵观 2023 年以来中国—东盟经贸合作，呈现以下亮点：**一是合作韧性强劲。**在世界经济复苏乏力、地缘政治影响外溢、贸易保护限制增多、世界主要经济体外贸普遍大幅下滑的情况下，中国—东盟双边贸易额仍保持 9000 亿美元以上高位。双方相互投资活跃，特别中国对东盟投资规模明显放大。**二是产业链供应链深度互嵌。**2023 年，中国对东盟进出口中间品 4.13 万亿元，占双边贸易额的 64.4%，东盟连续

多年保持中国中间品第一大贸易伙伴地位。**三是新动力不断涌现**。中国出口东盟的"新三样"产品即以电动载人汽车、锂电池、太阳能电池为代表的绿色低碳产品增长迅速。2023 年中国品牌占东盟新能源汽车销量 67%。风电、水电、太阳能等清洁能源合作规模持续扩大。**四是制度型开放取得新进展**。双方稳步推进区域内规则、规制、管理、标准等制度型开放合作，中国—东盟自贸区 3.0 版谈判加快，东盟国家标准化合作交流中心在南宁落地，中越友谊关—友谊智慧口岸建设启动。

当前中国—东盟经贸合作存在的难点：**一是货物贸易不平衡仍然存在**。2023 年中国对新加坡和越南的贸易差额均超过 450 亿美元，中国对马来西亚的贸易逆差超过 150 亿美元。**二是产业链供应链合作面临挑战**。发达国家制造业回流使中国—东盟制造业在全球产业链中的"链位"提升难度加大。**三是数字经济合作有待完善**。当前中国与东盟数字经济合作存在内容完整性不足、内容准确性不够、统一区域合作难度大等问题。**四是经贸提质增量需突破制度藩篱**。在双方经贸合作中还存在畅通口岸物流有堵点、跨境人民币结算不便利、运输标准和规则不统一等问题。

三、2025 年中国—东盟经贸合作展望

2025 年是东盟共同体建成 10 周年。随着中国—东盟全面战略伙伴关系深入发展，双方经贸合作有望延续快速发展势头。

一是贸易规模有望扩大。双方产业互嵌不断加深，在发展绿色经济、数字经济等方面具有共同的利益诉求，均高度重视经济的转型升级，积极培育经济增长新引擎，经贸合作的动力十足，空间广阔。预

计 2025 年双边贸易额将突破 1 万亿美元。以"新三样"为代表的绿色产品贸易将持续增长，数字贸易将成为双方合作新亮点。

二是相互投资前景广阔。东盟国家在交通、能源、通信等基础设施建设领域的需求持续扩大，为双方投资合作提供了巨大商机。全球产业链的重构将使双方产业链供应链合作更加紧密，带动双方在各自优势产业及其上下游产业的投资合作。如中国吉利汽车在与马来西亚宝腾汽车合资取得成功的基础上，计划再投资 100 亿美元在马来西亚丹绒马林打造汽车制造中心。

三是服务贸易提质增量。随着更多的国际航班逐步恢复和互免签证政策的落实，双方旅游合作有望恢复到疫情前水平。国际陆海贸易新通道骨干工程平陆运河加快建设，北部湾国际门户港功能不断完善，中国—东盟多式联运合作持续加强，将带动双方在港口、铁路等国际运输服务领域的合作。中国与东盟的规则、规制、管理、标准等制度型开放合作稳步扩大，将带动双方金融、数字贸易、软件服务、国际教育等服务贸易各领域走向深入。

四是自贸区 3.0 版落地见效。随着中国—东盟自贸区 3.0 版谈判的收官，本地区贸易投资自由化水平进一步提升，拓展了数字经济、绿色经济等新兴领域务实合作，形成更加包容、现代、全面和互利的中国—东盟自贸区。2025 年举办的第 22 届中国—东盟博览会将着力推动中国—东盟自贸区 3.0 版落地见效，让双方企业共享高水平自贸区带来的实惠，共享中国—东盟命运共同体建设的硕果。

一、2023 年以来中国—东盟经贸合作情况

2023 年中国—东盟经贸合作快速发展。货物贸易保持高位水平，投资合作持续强劲，服务贸易扩大开放，中国—东盟自贸区 3.0 版谈判加快推进。

（一）货物贸易保持高位水平

1. 规模

2023 年中国—东盟货物贸易进出口总额较 2022 年稍有回落，为 9114.72 亿美元，相比 2022 年下降了 4.9%。其中，中国自东盟进口 3879.24 亿美元，同比下降 4.8%。2023 年中国向东盟出口货物贸易额为 5510.46 亿美元，较 2022 年下降了 274.98 亿美元（见图 1）。

2. 商品结构

中国出口东盟的"新三样"产品即以电动载人汽车、锂电池、太阳能电池为代表的绿色低碳产品在 2022 年、2023 年成为中国—东盟货物贸易的亮点。2022 年，中国对东盟的"新三样"产品出口额强劲增长，2023 年出口额首次突破 110 亿美元（见表 1）。

单位：亿美元

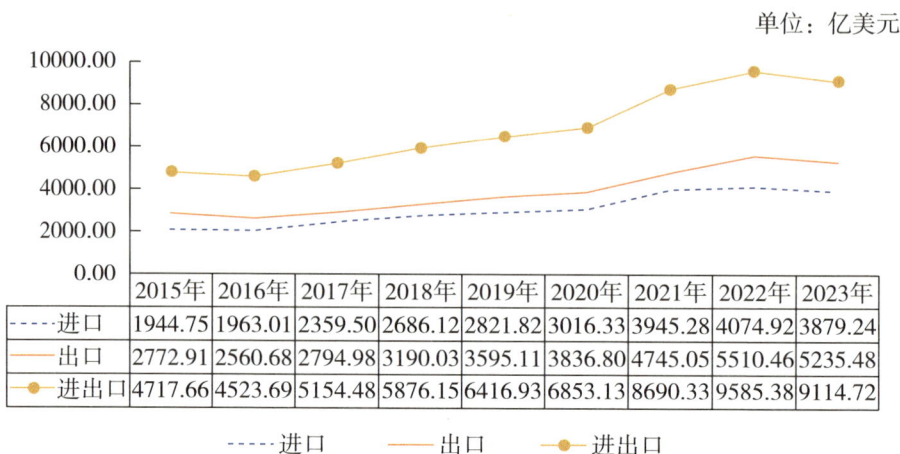

	2015年	2016年	2017年	2018年	2019年	2020年	2021年	2022年	2023年
进口	1944.75	1963.01	2359.50	2686.12	2821.82	3016.33	3945.28	4074.92	3879.24
出口	2772.91	2560.68	2794.98	3190.03	3595.11	3836.80	4745.05	5510.46	5235.48
进出口	4717.66	4523.69	5154.48	5876.15	6416.93	6853.13	8690.33	9585.38	9114.72

----- 进口　　—— 出口　　—●— 进出口

图 1　2015—2023 年中国—东盟货物贸易额

数据来源：中华人民共和国海关总署。

表 1　2021—2023 年中国—东盟"新三样"产品的贸易额与增长率

年份	进口额 （千美元）	出口额 （千美元）	进出口额 （千美元）	进出口额同比 增长率 （%）
2021	1535381.91	5685844.16	7221226.07	——
2022	2676201.97	8206394.42	10882596.39	50.70%
2023	1362423.44	11464593.93	12827017.37	17.87%

数据来源：中华人民共和国海关总署。

3. 国别分布特征

2023 年中国—东盟货物贸易额排在前三位的分别是越南、马来西亚和印度尼西亚，且无论是进口还是出口，排名前两位都是越南和马来西亚，可见两国是中国在东盟中主要贸易伙伴（见表2）。

表2　2023 年中国对东盟各国的货物贸易额及排序

序号	国家	进出口额（千美元）
1	越南	229793472.77
2	马来西亚	190243547.63
3	印度尼西亚	139415895.91
4	泰国	126279946.13
5	新加坡	108393419.38
6	菲律宾	71909581.03
7	缅甸	20949404.81
8	柬埔寨	14822297.93
9	老挝	7102232.58
10	文莱	2804681.89

数据来源：中华人民共和国海关总署。

4. 贸易差额

2023 年中国处于贸易顺差地位的贸易伙伴国为缅甸、菲律宾、新加坡、泰国、越南和柬埔寨，处于贸易逆差地位的贸易伙伴国为印度尼西亚、马来西亚、文莱和老挝（见表3）。

表3　2023 年中国与东盟各国的货物贸易差额

国家	出口额（千美元）	进口额（千美元）	贸易差额（千美元）
缅甸	11401673.88	9547730.90	1853942.98
印度尼西亚	65200435.56	74215460.00	-9015024.44
马来西亚	87382851.94	102860696.00	-15477844.06
菲律宾	52413350.81	19496230.00	32917120.81
新加坡	76963629.70	31429790.00	45533839.70
泰国	75736059.56	50543887.00	25192172.56
越南	137611635.00	92181838.00	45429797.00
文莱	857608.11	1947073.80	-1089465.69

续表

国家	出口额 （千美元）	进口额 （千美元）	贸易差额 （千美元）
老挝	3348297.04	3753935.5	−405638.46
柬埔寨	12752000.75	2070297.2	10681703.55

数据来源：中华人民共和国海关总署。

（二）双向投资强劲增长

1. 规模

2023年中国对东盟直接投资规模达173.06亿美元，在东盟外资来源地中排名第四，占东盟全年吸收外资的7.50%，占中国对外直接投资流量11.71%。2022年东盟对中国的投资再创新高，投资规模同比增长12.58%，达到119.08亿美元，东盟是中国第二大外资来源地，占中国实际利用外资规模的6.29%（见图2、3）。

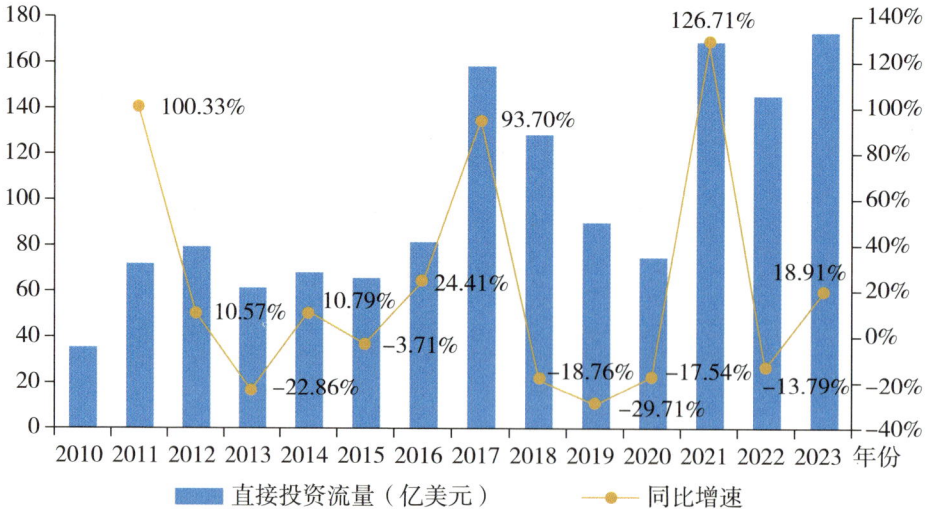

图2　2010—2023年中国对东盟直接投资规模及增速

数据来源：东盟秘书处、中国商务部。

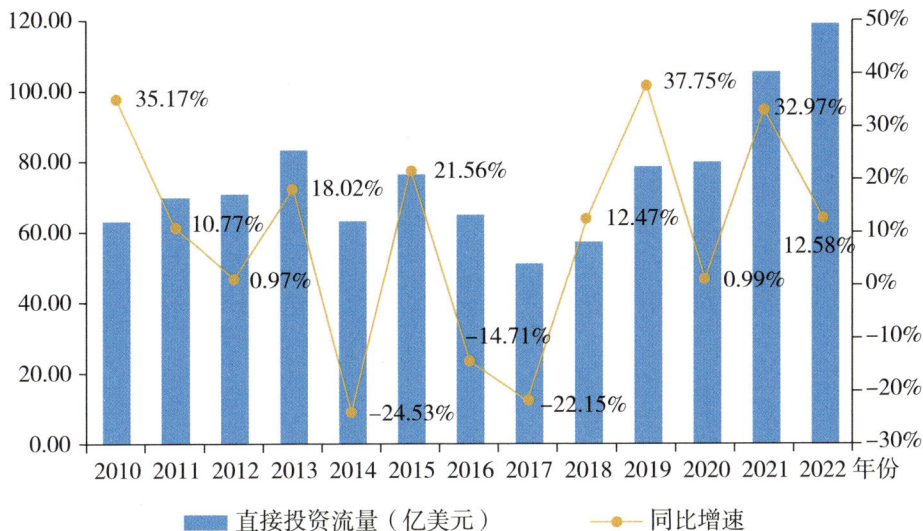

图 3　2010—2022 年东盟对中国直接投资规模及增速

数据来源：中国国家统计局。

2. 行业分布

2023 年，中国对东盟直接投资主要集中于制造业、批发和零售贸易及机动车辆和摩托车修理、房地产业等行业。其中，制造业投资 62.53 亿美元，同比增长 11.63%；批发和零售贸易、机动车辆和摩托车修理投资 36.16 亿美元，同比增长 77.12%；房地产业投资 32.12 亿美元，同比增长 42.51%（见表 4）。

表 4　2022 年和 2023 年中国对东盟直接投资的行业分布情况

行业	2022 年		2023 年	
	流量（百万美元）	比重（%）	流量（百万美元）	比重（%）
农林渔业	76.9	0.5	79.8	0.5

行业	2022 年		2023 年	
	流量 （百万美元）	比重 （%）	流量 （百万美元）	比重 （%）
采矿业	61.6	0.4	146.4	0.8
制造业	5602.0	38.5	6253.3	36.1
电、煤气、蒸汽和空调供应	425.5	2.9	837.6	4.8
供水；污水处理、废物管理和补救活动	-1.7	0.0	-10.8	-0.1
建筑业	605.6	4.2	696.2	4.0
批发和零售贸易；机动车辆和摩托车修理	2041.6	14.0	3616.1	20.9
运输和存储	498.7	3.4	465.6	2.7
住宿和餐饮业	82.9	0.6	67.0	0.4
信息和通信业	260.4	1.8	182.4	1.1
金融和保险业	2169.7	14.9	1401.9	8.1
房地产业	2253.9	15.5	3212.1	18.6
专业和科技活动	61.1	0.4	-102.4	-0.6
企业管理和商务服务业	-3.9	0.0	14.0	0.1
公共行政和国防；强制性社会保障	0.0	0.0	5.3	0.0
教育	22.3	0.2	1.0	0.0
卫生和社会福利业	0.2	0.0	23.5	0.1
艺术、娱乐和文娱活动	-1.7	0.0	-0.3	0.0
其他服务活动	398.6	2.7	416.9	2.4
其他行业	0.0	0.0	0.0	0.0
合计	14553.6	100.0	17305.7	100.0

数据来源：东盟统计司。

3. 国别结构

2023 年中国对东盟的直接投资主要流向新加坡、越南、印度尼西亚和柬埔寨（见表 5）。从东盟对中国直接投资看，新加坡占据绝对的龙头地位，2020—2022 年新加坡在东盟对中国的直接投资中平均占比超过 90%。

表 5　2021—2023 年中国对东盟直接投资的国别结构

国家	2021 年		2022 年		2023 年	
	流量（百万美元）	比重（%）	流量（百万美元）	比重（%）	流量（百万美元）	比重（%）
新加坡	6532.30	38.69	5825.60	40.03	7152.00	41.33
其他（以越南为主）	2207.19	13.07	2017.23	13.86	3412.63	19.72
柬埔寨	1176.51	6.97	1508.40	10.36	1991.41	11.51
印度尼西亚	5075.71	30.06	3510.51	24.12	1674.47	9.68
泰国	1361.96	8.07	945.91	6.50	1567.53	9.06
马来西亚	495.57	2.94	837.50	5.75	889.49	5.14
缅甸	15.25	0.09	-107.26	-0.74	602.14	3.48
菲律宾	18.53	0.11	15.69	0.11	15.99	0.09
合计	16883.01	100	14553.58	100	17305.66	100

数据来源：东盟秘书处。

（三）服务贸易加速扩张

2001 年，中国—东盟自贸区建设进程启动，双方于 2007 年签署了《服务贸易协议》，各国以正面清单方式达成了第一批服务市场开放承诺，对服务贸易各个部门做出了具体的开放承诺。中国—东盟服务贸易壁垒降低，双边服务贸易规模迅速增长，从 2007 年的 186.95 亿美元增长至 2011 年的 324.02 亿美元，年均增速达 19.09%[①]。2011 年，中国—东盟在第一批具体承诺的基础上签订了第二批服务贸易开放的具体承诺，在第一批服务贸易开放承诺的基础上进一步开放服务贸易市场。中国—东盟第二批服务贸易承诺的开放广度、深度均得到显著提升，中国—东盟服务贸易壁垒大大降低，双边服务贸易规模由 2011 年的 324.02 亿美元上升至 2021 年的 726.66 亿美元，年均增速达 9.95%[②]。2022 年，RCEP 正式生效，以负面清单方式承诺服务贸易进一步开放，中国—东盟服务贸易迎来新发展。

因双边服务贸易数据的更新较为滞后，最新数据仅更新到 2021 年，结合中国—东盟对外服务贸易数据，中国—东盟服务贸易发展呈现出以下特点：

1. 规模

中国、东盟各国的服务贸易规模迅速增长，呈现出巨大的发展活力和发展潜力。2023 年，中国服务贸易规模达 9331 亿美元，同比增长 4.95%[③]；东盟服务贸易规模达 10576.53 亿美元，同比增长 6.66%[④]，东盟国家服务贸易规模高速增长，服务贸易潜力巨大。以 2007—2023 年数据来看，中国服务贸易年均增速达 10.04%，东盟服务贸易年均增速达 8.58%，远高于世界服务贸易 5.94% 的年均增速，中国与东盟的对外服务贸易呈现出巨大的发展活力[⑤]。

---

① 数据来源：WTO Stats，https://timeseries.wto.org。
② 数据来源：WTO Stats，https://timeseries.wto.org。
③ 数据来源：中国商务部，http://www.mofcom.gov.cn。
④ 数据来源：东盟秘书处，https://data.aseanstats.org。
⑤ 数据来源：根据中国商务部、东盟秘书处、WTO Stats 数据库数据计算。

中国—东盟双向服务贸易规模日益扩大，互为重要的服务贸易合作伙伴。如图 4 所示，2010—2021 年中国—东盟双边服务贸易规模从 270.1 亿美元扩大到 726.66 亿美元，增长 269%，年均增速达 9.95%。其中中国从东盟进口规模从 150.48 亿美元上升至 392.94 亿美元，增长 261%，年均增速达 9.84%；对东盟出口规模从 119.62 亿美元上升至 333.72 亿美元，增长 279%，年均增速达 10.17%。

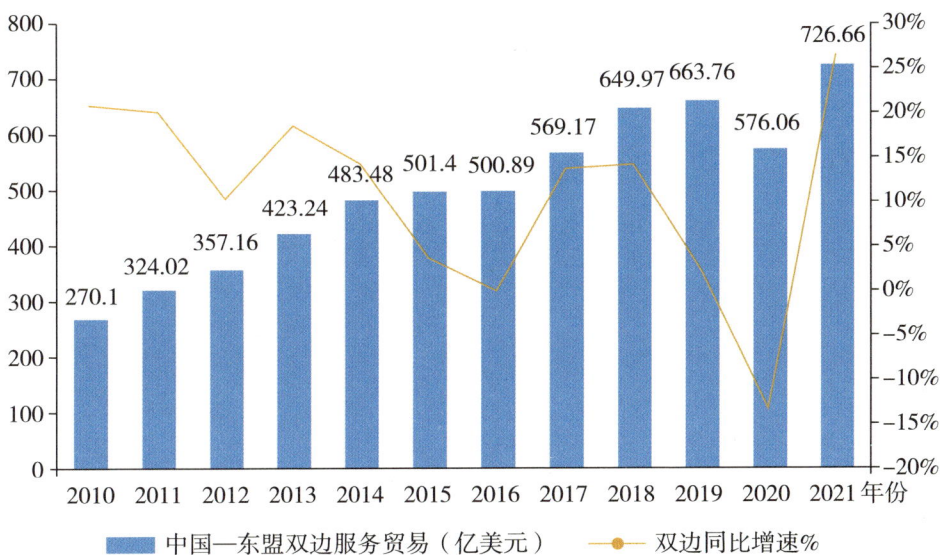

图 4　2010—2021 年中国—东盟双边服务贸易规模

数据来源：WTO Stats。

由表 6 可知，中国对东盟国家的服务贸易进出口基本处于逆差状态，且在疫情前处于逆差不断扩大的状态，疫情后逆差急剧缩小。2021 年，中国对东盟出口规模达 333.72 亿美元，同比上升 25.25%，占同期中国服务贸易出口规模的 11.22%。同年中国从东盟国家进口的服务贸易规模达 392.94 亿美元，同比上升 26.14%，占同期中国对外服务进口总额的 10.87%。2011 年至 2021 年，中国从东盟进口的服务贸易规模呈现上升趋势，中国从东盟的服务贸易进口年均增速达 9.84%，高于世界服务贸易进口增速。受疫情影响在 2020 年出现短暂下降，至 2021 年已恢复疫情前水平。

表6　2010—2021年中国对东盟服务贸易进出口

年份	出口（亿美元）	进口（亿美元）	差额（亿美元）
2010	119.62	150.48	-30.86
2011	144.41	179.61	-35.2
2012	157.75	199.41	-41.66
2013	191.43	231.81	-40.38
2014	215.99	267.49	-51.5
2015	217.49	283.91	-66.42
2016	215.25	285.64	-70.39
2017	242.68	326.49	-83.81
2018	265.89	384.08	-118.19
2019	280	383.76	-103.76
2020	266.44	309.62	-43.18
2021	333.72	392.94	-59.22

数据来源：WTO Stats。

2. 部门结构

中国—东盟间的服务产业具有相似性和互补性。双方的服务贸易仍以传统的服务部门为主，近年来新兴的服务部门贸易份额不断上升，占比不断提高，具有巨大的发展空间和发展潜力。

由图5、图6可以看到出口方面，中国对东盟出口集中在传统的运输、旅游、其他商业服务等传统部门，电信、计算机和信息服务出口规模和占比不断上升，金融服务出口占比不断提高，但规模有限。2019 年，中国对东盟服务贸易出口达 280 亿美元，集中在运输、其他商业服务、旅游、建筑四个部门，合计占中国对东盟服务贸易总出口的比例超过 80%。受疫情影响，2020 年中国对东盟服务贸易出口略微下降，到 2021 年已恢复到疫情前水平，2021 年中国对东盟服务贸易出口规模达 333.72 亿美元，同比上升 25.25%，集中在运输、其他商业服务、建筑、电信、计算机和信息服务四个部门，占比分别为 38.10%、24.73%、13.43%、10.06%。由于疫情影响，世界旅游服务出口大幅萎缩，中国对东盟的旅游服务贸易出口也由 2019 年的 17.99% 下降到 2021 年的 3.65%，同时运输部门占比迅速上升。

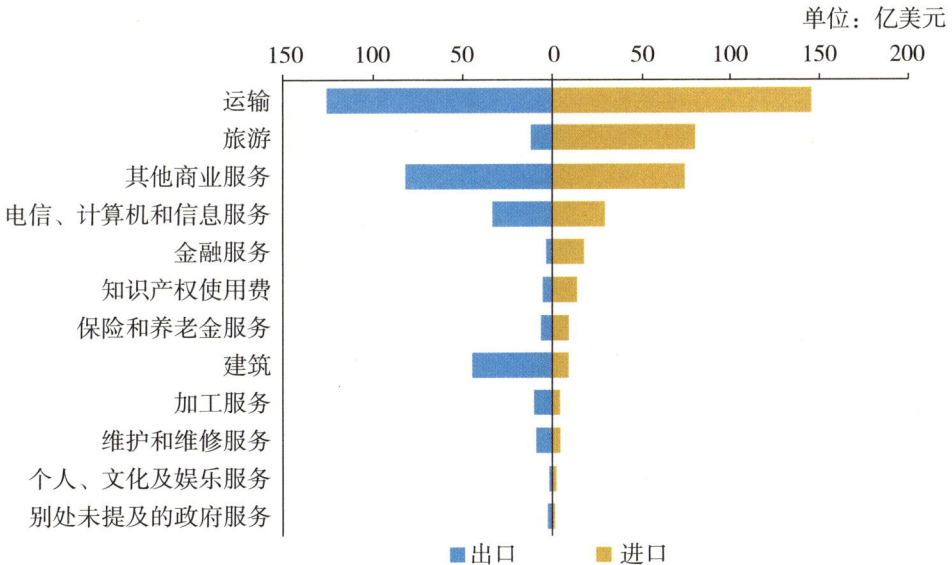

图 5　2021 年中国对东盟分部门服务贸易进出口

数据来源：WTO Stats。

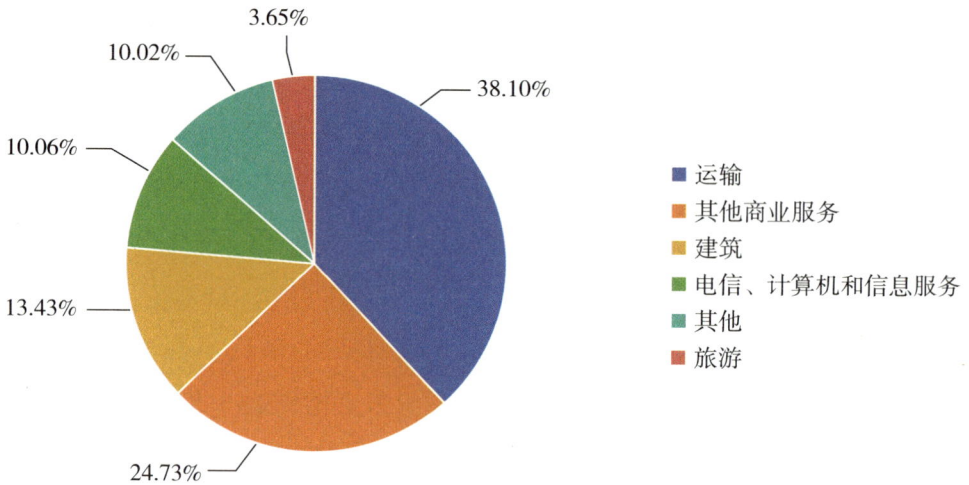

图 6　2021 年中国对东盟服务贸易出口各部门情况

数据来源：WTO Stats。

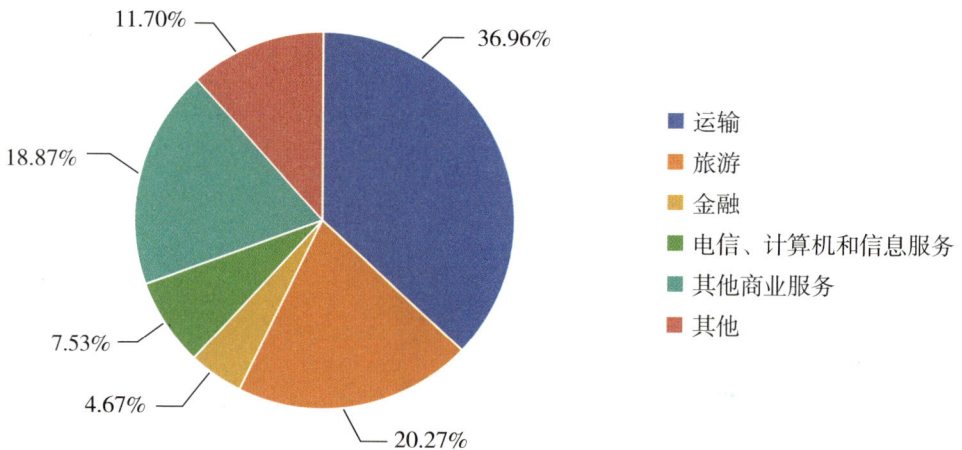

图 7　2021 年中国从东盟服务贸易进口的部门情况

数据来源：WTO Stats。

由图 5、图 7 可以看到进口方面，东盟对中国的出口服务主要集中在运输、旅游和其他商业服务部门。受疫情影响，东盟旅游服务出口严重受挫，东盟国家对中国的旅游服务出口占比由 2019 年的52.91%下降到 2021 年的 20.27%，同时运输部门对中国的服务贸易出口规模迅速扩大，从 2019 年的 88.32 亿美元上升至 2021 年的 145.22亿美元。其他商业服务出口同比增长 62.59%，达到 74.16 亿美元。

3. 国别结构

由表 7 可知，中国对东盟国家的服务贸易进出口国家较为集中，以新加坡、泰国、菲律宾和越南为主。其中新加坡占比最高，2021 年中国对新加坡出口额达 159.78 亿美元，进口 237.34 亿美元，是中国服务贸易出口的第三大贸易目的地，仅次于中国香港和美国。分进出口看，中国对东盟国家的进出口呈现出不一样的特点。

出口方面，中国对东盟服务贸易出口规模不断增长，但区域内不同国家的占比极不平衡。中国在东盟的服务贸易出口主要集中在新加坡、泰国、马来西亚和越南，占比分别为 47.88%、13.09%、11.85%、11.20%。且疫情后新加坡和越南的占比出现上升，马来西亚的占比出现下降。这是因为中国对新加坡的服务贸易出口主要集中在运输、其他商业服务以及电信、计算机和信息服务三个部门，受疫情的影响较小；越南承接中国以及发达国家的产业转移，基建需求以及制造业服务的需求较大。受疫情影响，中国对泰国、马来西亚的旅游服务出口迅速下降，运输服务的比例则大幅上升。中国对印度尼西亚、菲律宾、缅甸、柬埔寨、文莱、老挝等东盟国家的服务贸易出口量呈现增长趋势，但出口规模仍较小，且集中在运输、建筑、其他商业服务等部门。

进口方面，新加坡是中国服务贸易进口的重要来源国，2021 年其对中国的服务贸易出口总额达 237.74 亿美元，占东盟国家对中国出口总额至 60.50%，为中国的第四大服务贸易进口来源国家或地区。泰国、马来西亚、越南、菲律宾对中国的服务贸易出口则集中在旅游部门，疫情后萎靡不振，服务贸易出口占比也相应地下降。

表 7　2021 年中国对东盟 10 国的服务贸易进出口

国别	出口（亿美元）	进口（亿美元）
新加坡	159.78	237.74
泰国	43.7	43.61
菲律宾	39.55	30.64
越南	37.38	27.14
印度尼西亚	28.63	23.79
马来西亚	16.61	21.63
缅甸	2.99	4.6
老挝	2.33	2.03
柬埔寨	1.94	1.23
文莱	0.81	0.53

数据来源：WTO Stats。

（四）中国—东盟自贸区 3.0 版谈判加快推进

中国—东盟自贸区（CAFTA）的成立与发展，是全球经济一体化背景下，中国与东盟国家为应对全球经济变革、促进自身经济发展而做出的重要战略选择。该自贸区的建立不仅促进了双方经贸往来的显著增强，提升了区域经济的整体实力和影响力，还为世界其他发展中国家提供了经济一体化和区域合作的成功典范。

20 世纪 90 年代以来，全球经济一体化加速推进，区域经济合作成为各国提升竞争力的重要途径。随着亚洲金融危机的爆发进一步凸显了加强区域合作、提升经济抗风险能力的重要性，加速了 CAFTA 的进程。此外，中国在 WTO 中展现出了高度的责任感和开放的姿态，为中国—东盟自贸区的建立奠定了坚实的基础。在此背景下，中国与东盟国家基于共同的发展需求和地理优势，开始探索建立自贸区的可能性。

1. CAFTA 1.0 版实施效果

2002 年，中国与东盟签署《全面经济合作框架协议》，启动自贸区建设。合作涵盖货物贸易、服务贸易与投资。2004 年《货物贸易协定》签署，区内各国大幅降低关税壁垒，促进商品流通，至 2018 年，中国—东盟双向贸易额达到 5878.7 亿美元，较《框架协议》签署前增长近 10 倍；2007 年《服务贸易协议》签订，双方不断深化服务领域合作，服务贸易额显著增长，2018 年，双边服务贸易总额达到 584.5 亿美元，较协议签署当年增长了 227.7%。；2009 年《投资协议》签署，双向投资持续增长，2010—2018 年，中国对东盟投资从 73 亿美元增长至超过 110 亿美元，于 2017 年达到峰值 136.2 亿美元。总的来说，中国与东盟经贸合作势头强劲，需持续加强合作，构建更稳定高效的经济关系。

2. CAFTA 2.0 版实施效果

2015 年 11 月 22 日，中国—东盟自贸区升级议定书正式签署，2019 年 10 月 22 日对所有成员全面生效，形成了中国—东盟自贸区 2.0 版。

在货物贸易领域，中国—东盟自贸区 2.0 版以原产地规则和贸易便利化措施为重点。在原产地规则上，降低了货物获得原产地资格的门槛，搭配更精确的格式和标注方法，提高了企业报关效率。在贸易便利化上，双方通过优化海关流程等方式降低企业的通关时间和成本。中国与东盟的双边贸易总额从 2019 年的 4.43 万亿元增长到 2023 年的 6.41 万亿元，增长率达到 44.70%。

在服务贸易和投资领域，中国在众多行业作出改进承诺，东盟各国在 8 个方面约 70 个分部门向中国作出了更高水平的开放承诺。在技术经济合作上，双方同意在原有基础上扩展超过 10 个领域，并为有关项目提供资金支持。

3. CAFTA 3.0 版升级原因

第一，进一步激发双向贸易投资潜能。2010—2023 年，中国与东盟之间的经贸关系显示出了较高的发展水平和强劲的发展潜力，13 年间贸易额年均增长 11.54%，超过中国年均进出口增速约 3.5 个百分点，中国—东盟进出口占全国比重从 9.85% 上涨至 15.36%，中国与东盟的贸易在国民经济中的地位不断提升。同时，中国与东盟之间高附加值产品贸易比重不断增加，服务贸易显著扩展。在当前世界经济环境面临诸多不确定性和挑战的背景下要进一步提升双方经济合作的韧性和稳定性、扩展合作领域、拓展合作深度、寻找新的经济增长点，对自贸区进行升级就显得尤为重要。

第二，推动区域经济一体化以应对全球挑战。当前全球经济增长放缓，贸易保护主义抬头，中国东盟要保持地区经济持续、高质量的增长，就必须持续增进区域经济合作。中国—东盟自贸区 3.0 版的升级将形成更紧密的命运共同体，推动建设更大规模的经济一体化，为区域发展提供稳定的外部环境。自贸区的升级可以使双方在更多的议题上达成共识，以更大的声量参与国际事务，在全球发展中掌握更大的主动权。

第三，更高级别多边经贸协定的挑战。随着多边贸易协定的陆续签署实施，中国—东盟自贸区既拥有持续发展的潜力又面临着被稀释的可能。在 RCEP 正式实施的背景下，原有的自贸区协定存在落后趋势。RCEP 彰显了双方推动区域经济一体化的坚定决心与共同利益追求，再加上更完善的规则体系，为中国—东盟自贸区未来发展的方向作出了重要的参考和借鉴。综上所述，RCEP 的正式实施为中国—东盟自贸区 3.0 版升级提供了实践基础和动力源泉，自贸区升级是必然选择。

第四，打造经济增长新引擎，共享新发展机遇。信息技术的飞跃推动数字经济成为全球经济增长的新引擎，与传统贸易存在较大差异。然而，自贸区成员国间数字经济水平差距较大、协定在相关规则上存在空白，导致双方在数字经济的合作中，往往面临着冲突和不确定性。因此，对中国—东盟自贸区进行"升级版"谈判迫在眉睫。

绿色经济已成为经济增长的重要动力。首先，加入绿色经济相关规则可以进一步降低中国和东盟国家之间的关税水平，同时打破相关非关税壁垒，实现贸易自由化的升级。其次，通过加强区内绿色基础设施建设合作，进一步提升贸易便利化。最后，中国和东盟国家可以借谈判机会，在相关方面开展更多的合作，激发区域内技术创新活力。

第五，中国—东盟自贸区升级惠及企业与民众。企业层面，升级带来稳定经贸环境，降低政策不确定性。在投资上，投资领域扩大，权益保护水平提高，产业合作不断加强。同时，自贸区升级将助力企业利用数字经济等新动能，增强竞争优势。此外，自贸区 3.0 版还有望在人员流动等方面提供便利，助力企业跨国经营。

民众层面，随着自贸区规则的升级，区域内优质产品加快流动，消费者将拥有更多选择优质产品的机会，满足更多元化的需求。此外，自贸区规则升级将带动更多产业的发展，为民众创造更多的就业机会，特别是在数字技术和绿色经济等领域。

4. CAFTA 3.0 版谈判展望

货物贸易：在关税上，提升关税减免水平，削减非关税壁垒。在原产地规则上，采取更简化和灵活的原产地标准；提高原产地证书申领便利化水平；加强与其他多边贸易协定的联动，提升规则一致性。在贸易便利化上，简化程序、降低合规成本、加快货物放行；加快建设标准化基础设施，提高货物的运输效率和安全性；开展口岸数字化建设，加快信息技术在贸易中的应用。

电子商务：首先，提升电子商务贸易便利化，接受电子文件形式，建立统一的电子认证与电子签名规范。其次，改善商务环境，加强信息保护，保护消费者权益。再次，打造一体化综合跨境电子商务平台，实现各职能部门高效对接，加快数据共享和流程优化。

数字经济合作：通过对标 RCEP 等高标准经贸规则，在加强数字基础设施建设的基础上，促进数据跨境流动；通过加速数字技术应用与贸易相结合，探索技术应用的新模式、新业态；进一步推动数字服务贸易，加快相关数字内容出口；加大数字知识产权保护力度和人才培养水平，提升区内创新能力和数字产业的健康发展。

绿色经济合作：双方在加强绿色技术的分享与合作的基础上，提升产业绿色水平；加快建立绿色标准与认证体系，提升标准的科学性和可操作性；在金融上，建立专门的绿色投融资机制和新型工具，为绿色项目提供保障；此外，双方也将明确目标和责任，通过共同制定碳中和行动计划，搭配碳交易市场，形成区域协同的低碳发展格局。

供应链互联互通：发布新的互联互通总体规划，提升供应链基础设施建设水平；持续加快相关基础设施与供应链数字化、绿色化建设，提升供应链的透明度、可追溯性和智能化水平，实现供应链的可持续发展；通过建立应急响应机制和风险预警系统，加强供应链风险管理，提升供应链韧性。

中小企业优惠政策：首先开展针对中小企业的自贸区规则培训，提升企业应对能力和市场竞争力。其次，减少政府的行政限制，确保中小企业在区域内外的市场享有公平待遇，禁止歧视性做法。在资金支持上，出台专属信贷政策，利用大数据等科技手段，降低融资成本。在法律保障上，强化区内法律交流，为中小企业提供必要的法律援助服务，提升企业法律意识，保障中小企业的自由竞争。

二、2023 年以来中国—东盟经贸合作评析

纵观 2023 年以来中国—东盟经贸合作，呈现以下亮点：一是合作韧性强劲，二是产业链供应链深度互嵌，三是新动力不断涌现，四是制度型开放取得新进展。当前，中国—东盟经贸合作的重点是互联互通走深走实、数字经济对接落地、绿色低碳高质量发展，存在的难点是货物贸易不平衡仍然存在、产业链供应链合作面临挑战、数字经济合作有待完善、经贸提质增量需突破制度藩篱。

（一）中国—东盟经贸合作亮点

1. 合作韧性强劲

贸易投资合作发展稳定。贸易方面，世界经济复苏乏力、地缘政治影响外溢、贸易保护限制增多、世界主要经济体外贸普遍大幅下滑的情况下，中国—东盟双边贸易额仍保持 9000 亿美元以上高位。2023 年，中国与东盟连续第 4 年互为最大贸易伙伴。投资方面，双方相互投资活跃，特别是中国对东盟投资规模明显放大。2023 年，中国对东盟投资增幅高达 44.6%，双向累计投资超过 3800 亿美元。东盟成为中国车企海外投资最为集中地区。2023 年中国品牌占东盟新能源汽车销量 67%。粤港澳大湾区、海南自贸港同东盟合作初见成效，海南自贸港东南亚投资中心正式运营。中国在东盟设立直接投资企业超过 6500

家，双方依托"两国双园"共建经贸创新发展示范园区，开辟了东盟国家融入中国地方开放发展的新通道。①

区域经济一体化日益加深。中国—东盟经贸合作的深化离不开自贸协定的制度性支撑。中国—东盟自贸区 3.0 版升级谈判正有序推进，已举行 7 轮磋商。中方与东盟各方共同努力，打造更高水平的自贸区。同时，《区域全面经济伙伴关系协定》（RCEP）生效两年多来，推动区域贸易成本大幅降低，产供链联系更为紧密，为成员国带来实实在在的收益。

发展援助合作不断加强。中国重点向柬埔寨、老挝、缅甸、越南等提供经济技术援助，支持东盟缩小内部发展差距和一体化发展，主要包括支持东盟国家建设基础设施项目，助推经济社会发展；开展减贫、卫生、抗灾等项目合作，增进东盟国家民生福祉；通过奖学金、短期培训等人力资源开发项目，帮助东盟国家培养各领域人才，增强自主发展能力。

2. 产业链供应链深度互嵌

2023 年，在中间品进出口方面，中国与东盟国家的贸易额为 4.13 万亿元，占双边贸易总额高达 64.4%，并且东盟连续多年保持中国中间品第一大贸易伙伴。② 中国—东盟产业链供应链的双向投资模式进一步发展，具体表现在以下几点：第一，贸易关系。双向投资模式促进了双方在制造业、农业、服务业等领域的合作，提升了贸易便利化水平，降低了贸易成本，从而增加了双边贸易额。例如，中国企业投

---

① 外交部网站. 2023 年中国对东盟投资增幅高达 44.6% ［EB/OL］.（2024-07-27）［2024-07-30］. https://investgo.cn/article/yw/tzyj/202407/732344.html.

② 经济观察网. 如何保持外贸韧性 ［EB/OL］.（2024-01-16）［2024-08-03］. https://www.163.com/dy/article/IOILP8B605118O92.html.

资东盟国家的基础设施建设，带动了相关设备和技术的出口，东盟国家的农产品和原材料出口到中国，满足了中国的市场需求。第二，投资结构。双向投资模式使得双方投资结构更加多元化，提高了投资效益。中国对东盟国家的投资主要集中在基础设施建设、房地产和制造业等领域，东盟国家对中国的投资主要集中在制造业、服务业和科技领域，这种互补性的投资结构有助于双方经济的协同发展。第三，和平稳定性。双向投资模式有助于增进双方的了解和互信，降低地缘政治风险，维护地区的和平稳定。通过经济合作，双方的国家利益更加紧密地联系在一起，有助于通过对话和合作解决争端。例如，中国与东盟国家的双向投资合作典范是新加坡，新加坡是中国在东盟国家最大的投资目的地，同时是东盟国家在中国最大投资来源国，双方在金融、物流、科技等领域开展广泛的合作，共同推动了双边贸易的发展。这种双向投资模式不仅促进了双方的经济发展，还有助于增进双方在国际事务中的合作，共同维护地区的和平稳定。[①]

3. 合作新动力不断涌现

首先，新能源产品贸易规模扩大。中国出口东盟的"新三样"产品即以电动载人汽车、锂电池、太阳能电池为代表的绿色低碳产品增长迅速。2023年中国品牌占东盟新能源汽车销量67%。风电、水电、太阳能等清洁能源合作规模持续扩大。其次，蓝色经济合作不断加强。2023年9月，中国—东盟领导人会议提出，要最大限度地发挥蓝色经济在实现经济增长、提高社会包容性、提升人民生活水平以及保护环境中的作用。2023年，中国海洋经济占GDP的比重是7.9%，提升空

---

① 任城区商务局. 中新经贸合作迎来新契机［EB/OL］.（2024-01-01）［2024-07-31］. http://www.rencheng.gov.cn/art/2024/1/1/art_73208_2780460.html.

间较大。中国对外贸易有 94% 以上通过海运实现，东盟通过海运实现的对外贸易则为 60%。中国与东盟之间的贸易有 65% 通过海运实现。此外，中国与东盟在数字经济方面互补性强、合作潜力巨大，数字经济合作将成为推动中国—东盟双边贸易增长的新动力。① 跨境电商作为贸易新业态、新模式，已成为增强中国—东盟经贸联系的重要因素，有效减轻了疫情对贸易的冲击。中国电商平台加快在东南亚国家建设海外仓的步伐，在 RCEP 生效、线上经济常态化背景下、加之政府支持和市场发力，中国和东盟跨境电商合作前景广阔。②

4. 中国—东盟制度型开放取得新进展

双方稳步推进区域内规则、规制、管理、标准等制度型开放合作，中国—东盟自贸区 3.0 版谈判加快，东盟国家标准化合作交流中心在南宁落地，中越友谊关—友谊智慧口岸建设启动。中国与东盟抓住数字经济发展机遇，打造适用于发展中国家的数字经贸和治理规则：一是利用既有的数字经济协定。RCEP、CPTPP 和 DEPA 均涵盖数字贸易规则，根据各自数字经济发展的进程和治理理念选择加入任一协定，增强加入协定的灵活性。通过参与这些协定，推动自身的数字经济发展，参与完善协定内容，指导未来的数字合作。这样有利于推动建立更公平、更平衡的国际数字经济关系，有助于各国掌握数字治理的主动权和话语权，避免在全球数字经济体系中被发达国家边缘化，或被迫接受一个高度自由化的数字经济体系。二是利用现有的数字合作方式。通过"数字丝绸之路"加强中国与东盟国家的数字经济合作，分

---

① 人民网. 中国东盟推动海洋经济合作正当时［EB/OL］.（2024-05-25）［2024-07-31］. http://www.people.com.cn/.

② 人民网. 中国东盟经贸合作持续深化 跨境电商成新引擎［EB/OL］.（2022-09-25）［2024-07-31］. http://www.people.com.cn/.

享各自在数字基础设施建设、电子商务发展和智慧城市建设等领域的技术和经验。

（二）中国—东盟经贸合作重点

1. 互联互通走深走实

中老铁路客货两旺，中老泰马跨境铁路班列正式开行，西部陆海新通道铁海联运班列推动各方产供链深度融合，中国—东盟互联互通走深走实。雅万高铁即雅加达至万隆高速铁路，是印尼和东南亚第一条高速铁路，也是中国与印尼务实合作的旗舰项目。雅万高铁的开通运营不仅改善了当地交通条件，方便沿线民众出行，同时还带动了商业开发和旅游产业发展，给区域经济社会的发展注入了新动能，是中印尼两国合作的重要标志。此外，雅万高铁的建设过程中，累计解决了当地5.1万人次的就业需求，培训印尼员工4.5万人次。[①]

2. 数字经济对接落地

中国—东盟双方持续完善经贸合作机制，中国—东盟博览会、中国—东盟商务与投资峰会、中国—东盟信息港等经贸平台等重要载体，极大促进了中国与东盟在数字相关领域的项目对接及落地合作。东盟市场吸引了一大批中国数字化领域的龙头企业快速布局，包括阿里、腾讯、京东等电商平台，蚂蚁集团等移动支付企业，以及华为、中兴通讯等数字企业。这些中国企业与Tokopedia、Lazada等东盟数字企业深度合作，推广互联网先进技术和成熟商业模式，带动东盟相关产业

[①] 新华社. 雅万高铁正式开通运营［EB/OL］.（2023-10-18）［2024-07-31］. http://www.xinhuanet.com/2023-10/18/c_1129923113.htm.

发展和数字互联互通建设。①

3. 绿色低碳高质量发展

中国与东盟在自然资源、生产能力和产业结构上各有所长，互补性强，是天然的绿色经济合作伙伴。中国政府贯彻绿色发展理念，积极发展生态环保、可持续能源等产业，构建绿色低碳循环发展经济体系，为中国与东盟开展绿色经济投资合作奠定坚实基础。近年来，双方大力推进循环经济、节能环保、绿色能源、可持续金融、应对气候变化等领域的政策对话与交流合作。

中国和东盟在新能源汽车领域互补优势显著，合作前景广阔。产业层面，东盟领导人已就发展区域电动汽车生态系统达成共识，各成员国相继出台相关产业投资激励政策，且部分成员国镍、稀土等资源储备丰富，开展产业链、供应链合作基础较好。消费层面，新加坡公布了绿色交通发展蓝图，泰国计划在 2030 年前实现纯电动汽车新车登记占比 50%，菲律宾要求国内公共交通企业将纯电动汽车使用比例提升到 5% 以上，印度尼西亚自 2023 年起推出电动汽车购车补贴，计划在 2025 年前将电动汽车销售份额提升至 25%。②

（三）中国—东盟经贸合作难点

1. 货物贸易不平衡仍然存在

2023 年中国对新加坡和越南的贸易差额均超过 450 亿美元，中国

---

① 潘强，朱丽莉. 数字赋能中国—东盟经贸合作［N/OL］. 经济参考报，2021-09-09［2024-07-31］.

② 参考消息. 东南亚借力中国发展电动汽车［EB/OL］.（2023-12-12）［2024-07-31］. https://www.163.com/dy/article/ILPH1FVM0514BQ68.html.

对马来西亚的贸易逆差超过 150 亿美元。中国重视与东盟贸易不平衡问题，积极采取多种措辞妥善解决，推动双边贸易健康发展，巩固新发展格局下与东盟的战略伙伴关系。

第一，继续推进贸易自由化便利化，扩大自东盟成员国的进口。一是继续单方面扩大对柬埔寨、老挝、缅甸等东盟成员国的零关税产品范围。二是高质量实施《区域全面经济合作伙伴关系协定》（RCEP）等自由贸易协定。充分利用自由贸易协定的规则和规制，特别是 RCEP 的原产地累积规则、90% 以上产品削减关税等，进一步扩大自东盟成员国的进口。三是继续发挥进口博览会、东博会、中国国际投资贸易洽谈会等会展平台作用。加强与东盟成员国的交流、合作和协商，可以丰富这些会展平台内容，设立或继续设立专门的东盟成员国产品展示平台，宣传其产品和服务，发挥中国国内超大规模的市场优势，有利于扩大东盟成员国产品对中国的出口。此外，继续推进贸易自由化和便利化，加强与东盟成员国的海关合作、资质互认等，促进通关便利和高效运作。

第二，继续倡导投资自由化便利化，增加中国对东盟投资规模。综合考量东亚文化、区位优势、产业转移规律等，中国率先对东盟成员国进行产业转移，增加对东盟投资规模；发挥投资与贸易联动效应，进一步增加自东盟成员国的进口，形成多方共赢的发展格局。充分运用双边、多边各项协定，帮助企业有效投资。此外，继续营造良好的和平发展环境，加强与东盟 200 多个友好城市的合作，在灾害管理、缩小发展差距、互联互通建设等领域开展项目合作，释放我国经济社会发展的红利，特别是疫情之后新格局下加快东盟成员国经济复苏进程。

第三，对标国际先进规则，高质量建设境外经贸合作区等。一是加强与东盟及其成员国的合作，高质量实施 RCEP 等，共同建设世界上人口最多、经贸规模最大、最具发展潜力的自贸区，推进贸易和投资的自由化和便利化，进一步释放出巨大效应。二是对标绿色发展、环境保护等高水平国际先进规则，积极建设自由贸易试验区和海南自由贸易港、境外经贸合作区等，加强这些特殊经济区之间的合作，有助于我国企业掌握国际规则，适应东盟成员国的规制要求和提升国际竞争力。三是进一步优化境外经贸合作区布局和发展规划，提高其运营质量，发挥与东盟成员国的货物贸易、服务贸易、投资合作互补优势，探索产业链、供应链、价值链深度融合的国际分工合作模式，夯实共建"一带一路"合作基础，进一步提升我国与东盟成员国的合作水平和质量。①

2. 产业链供应链合作面临挑战

发达国家制造业回流使中国—东盟制造业在全球产业链中的"链位"提升难度加大。东盟开始成为维护区域产业链供应链安全的重要主体。目前，中国与东盟形成了"东盟向中国出口初级品—从中国进口机械设备（资本密集型）和中间品（技术密集型）—再将消费品（劳动密集型）出口给中国和第三国"的互利共赢的"区域循环"模式。此外，东盟在能源、矿产、农业等领域有着明显的比较优势，因此增强并优化中国—东盟产业链供应链具有迫切性。双方需开放共建更有韧性的中国—东盟产业链供应链，以稳定中国—东盟产业链供应

① 中国经济时报. 多方式解决与东盟贸易不平衡问题 ［EB/OL］.（2023-05-15）［2024-07-31］. http://fta.mofcom.gov.cn/article/chinadongmengupgrade/chinadong-mengupgradegfguandian/202305/539251.html.

链为重点，务实推进向东盟的主动开放进程。这个进程以实现中国—东盟自由贸易的重大突破为目标，以提升产业链供应链融合度与可持续为重点，以现有区域和次区域合作机制与基础设施网络为依托，以分国别、分步骤推进为基本策略。例如，在货物贸易领域率先实施，并向服务贸易拓展；在陆域领域率先实施，并向海洋领域拓展；在经贸领域率先实施，并向社会领域拓展。①

3. 数字经济合作有待完善

当前，中国与东盟数字经济合作主要规则在具体实施过程中仍存在不足。一是内容完整性不足。数字经济内容集中于电子商务一章，仅包括数字经济发展的基础性规定，未涉及数字产品、数字技术和源代码等数字经济新兴的重要议题。二是内容准确性不够。RCEP 既强调数据跨境传输，又重视数据自由流动与国家主权安全的平衡，但具体的数据跨境传输实施细节仍然处于模糊状态，因此，在实际操作过程中仍然面临诸多风险和难题。三是统一区域合作难度大。RCEP 作为规模最大的自由贸易协定，仅就东盟内部 10 个成员国来说，数字经济发展理念不一，发展进程各异，统一区域的内部数字经济合作理念和发展措施是一个重大关卡。

中国与东盟的数字经济合作要以既有的数字经贸规则为主导，完善合作方式、深化合作内容，又要推动协商签订"中国—东盟数字经济合作协定"，以提高合作的精确度。中国与东盟应抓住数字经济发展机遇，打造出适用于发展中国家的数字经贸和治理规则，突破霸权国家不公平的垄断和压迫，营造公平、可持续的数字发展环境，发出

---

① 光明网. 做强中国—东盟产业链供应链 [EB/OL]. (2023-12-10) [2024-07-31]. https://news.gmw.cn/2023-12-10/content_37017845.htm.

自己的声音，在找到属于发展中国家的数字发展道路的同时惠及全球发展中国家。中国作为共建"一带一路"倡议的发起者，可通过"数字丝绸之路"加强与共建国家的数字经济合作，分享其在数字基础设施建设、电子商务发展和智慧城市建设等领域的技术和经验。

4. 经贸提质增量需突破制度藩篱

在双方经贸合作中还存在畅通口岸物流有堵点、跨境人民币结算不便利、运输标准和规则不统一等问题。首先，随着 RCEP 政策红利不断释放，中国面向东盟的跨境电商交易规模不断扩大，亟须打通多式联运堵点，提升货物流转效率。在转关环节进行业务创新，实现"无感式"转关模式，全程转关无纸化作业、电子关锁自动解锁、转关数据自动核销等，将大幅提升货物运输时效。针对市场痛点堵点，推动贸易便利化改革，培育发展贸易新业态，加快形成面向东盟的跨境电商产业集聚区。其次，清算模式存在弊端，跨境清算效率有待提升。离岸人民币来源不足，境外投资渠道缺乏，限制了跨境人民币业务的市场发展规模。① 此外，制度创新，是双方经贸合作中的运输标准和规则统一的核心任务。中国（广西）自由贸易试验区（简称广西自贸试验区）聚焦面向东盟、服务西部陆海新通道、沿边开放三大特色，积极开展差异化探索和特色制度创新，已探索形成 5 批共 169 项自治区级制度创新成果。②

---

① 中国外汇网. 中国与东盟地区跨境人民币业务风险防范［EB/OL］.（2019-12-23）［2024-07-31］. http://shop.chinaforex.com.cn/magazine/pages/dgarticle.vc?article=48608.

② 广西日报官网. 广西自贸试验区改革试验田收获新"丰"景［EB/OL］.（2024-5-29）［2024-07-31］. http://www.gxrb.com.cn.

三、2025 年中国—东盟经贸合作展望

（一）货物贸易

1. 持续扩大中国—东盟贸易合作规模

中国与东盟国家的经济具有明显互补性，为双边贸易合作奠定了坚实基础。在产业链、供应链、市场需求等层面，双方具有广泛一致性。同时，双方在绿色经济、数字经济等新兴领域拥有共同的利益追求，均高度重视经济的转型升级，积极寻求新的经济增长点。经贸合作的动力强劲，空间广阔。

RCEP 政策的深入落实以及中国—东盟自贸区 3.0 版本的快速推进，创造了更有发展前景的贸易预期，为释放双方贸易潜力创造了良好条件。一方面，RCEP 等政策的深入实施，根据贸易转移效应，中国与东盟经济体之间的供应链网络将更具韧性，双方之间的贸易关系更加稳定；另一方面，双方积极推进自贸区建设，破除贸易合作的各种壁垒，发挥超大市场规模效应，进一步扩展贸易合作的广度与深度，开辟更为广阔的合作空间。

中国正在加快构建全国统一大市场，深化要素市场化改革，对接高标准国际经贸规则，不断为中国—东盟经贸合作注入新的活力。东盟国家内部也积极推进国内经济体制改革，加大经济开放力度，为对

外经贸合作创造良好的国内市场环境，切实推动中国—东盟贸易合作不断深化。

2. 深化"新三样"产品为代表的中国—东盟绿色贸易合作

东盟国家积极推进新能源汽车（NEV）行业的发展。马来西亚计划 2025 年在全国范围内建立约 1 万个公共充电设施，到 2030 年实现电动车在该国汽车总销量中占比 15%；泰国政府降低了新能源汽车整车和零部件进口关税，并为购买者提供车辆购置补贴等；印度尼西亚则提出打造东南亚电动汽车制造和出口枢纽的目标，力争到 2035 年将电动汽车产量提高到 100 万辆。这些措施为中国与东盟开展绿色贸易合作提供了广阔的市场空间与有力的政策支持。

在光伏领域，越南政府于 2024 年 4 月 1 日批准发布《第八个电力发展规划》（PDP VIII），旨在到 2030 年显著扩增光伏电站规模及储能能力。菲律宾政府将可再生能源、储能等绿色生态系统行业纳入"外资优先投资行业"，并给予不同程度和期限的税收优惠。能源转型这一目标的实现，需要资金、技术和基础设施的支持，而中国光伏组件产量已连续 16 年位居全球榜首，多晶硅、硅片、电池片、组件等产量与产能的全球占比均超过 80%，具有明显的技术与成本优势。这为中国与东盟在新能源领域合作奠定了基础，双方优势互补，合作潜力巨大。

在新能源电池领域，中国汽车工业协会公布的数据显示，中国申请的动力电池专利占全球 74%，已成为全球锂电池及固态电池领域主要技术来源国之一。比亚迪、宁德时代等中国企业在开发新能源电池方面的技术优势明显。得益于技术的累积与升级效应，未来中国在新能源等绿色经济领域的国际技术竞争力会进一步加强，这一趋势为中国与东盟国家深化绿色贸易合作奠定了坚实的基础，提供了强大的技术驱动力。

3. 积极推进中国—东盟数字贸易合作

中国发挥在数字技术、数字基础设施方面的优势，对东盟国家中缺乏数字化条件的落后地区，实施精准的信息与技术援助。通过定制化方案，不仅完善这些地区的硬件设施，还推动信息模式的革新，构建起融合多元技术、系统高度兼容的数字基础设施体系。这将从根本上解决当前合作中普遍存在的互联互通水平低下、信息孤岛现象严重等问题，促进中国—东盟数字贸易合作的持续发展。

中国与东盟将继续构建包括跨境电商平台、供应链管理平台、物流平台、企业销售 APP 在内的完整、高效的数字贸易生态体系，为双方开展数字贸易合作提供坚实的平台支撑。同时，双方要大力建设数字化跨境物流通道，打造数字贸易物流服务中心，推进通关、运输全过程数字化。比如未来双方可合作探索搭建高效的数字化物流信息协同大平台，利用云计算、物联网、大数据等技术，对接国内外的物流企业系统、外贸综合服务平台和海关信息服务平台等，即时提供全主体、全环节、全天候的物流信息服务，切实提升跨境的物流效率，加快实现高水平互联互通。

中国与东盟未来应该积极参与全球数字贸易规则谈判，提升在双方数字贸易规则中的话语权。同时，中国与东盟开展数字贸易合作时，要积极分享自身的数字贸易治理经验，以助力东盟国家数字贸易制度体系的完善，不断优化中国—东盟数字贸易合作框架，推进中国与东盟数字贸易合作持续深入发展。

（二）双向投资

1. 全球产业链供应链调整创造投资新契机

当前，全球产业链供应链加速调整，东盟成为维护区域产业链供应链安全的重要主体，中国与东盟在产业链供应链上逐渐形成互利共赢的"区域循环"模式。2023 年，中国与东盟贸易额占我国贸易总额的比重为 15.3%。其中，中间品进出口占双边进出口总额的 64.4%。东盟国家在能源、矿产、农业等领域的比较优势以及经济的多样性为寻求供应链多元化的中国合作伙伴提供了广泛的选择。预期 2024 年，中国—东盟在产业链供应链中互为比较优势的行业将成为双边投资的热点。

2. RCEP 全面生效释放服务业投资需求

2023 年《区域全面经济伙伴关系协定》（RCEP）在东盟国家开始全面生效，根据协定，各成员国将在 15 年内逐步开放 65% 以上的服务部门，包括金融、通讯、教育、医疗、旅游、文化等多个领域，这为中国与东盟在服务业领域的双向投资创造了巨大的机会。预期 2025年，随着 RCEP 的深入实施，中国与东盟在服务业领域的双向投资将进一步扩大和深化。双方在金融、教育、医疗、旅游、文化和 ICT 等领域的合作，将为区域经济增长和社会发展注入新的动力。

3. 基础设施领域投资潜力巨大

当前，东盟各国正积极推进基础设施现代化建设，基础设施建设存在巨大潜力。根据国际货币基金组织（IMF）的预测，到 2024 年，东盟国家的基础设施投资需求将达到约 2.1 万亿美元，这为中国—东盟双边合作提供了巨大的市场空间。与此同时，中国拥有丰富的基础设施建设经验和技术优势，在高铁、港口、能源电网等基建领域具备世界领先的竞争力，充分满足了东盟推进基础设施建设现代化的需求。预期 2025 年，中国与东盟在基础设施领域的投资将进一步深化，中国企业在资金、技术、管理等方面的优势将与东盟国家的市场、资源等优势相结合，广泛参与到东盟国家的基础设施建设项目中，共同推动区域基础设施的升级和完善，进一步推进互联互通和区域一体化进程。

4. 数字经济合作方兴未艾

根据麦肯锡的预测，到2025年，东盟国家的数字经济规模将达到约1万亿美元，占地区GDP的比重将超过20%。与此同时，中国拥有世界上最大的互联网用户群体和高度发达的数字基础设施，在电子商务、移动支付、人工智能和大数据等领域具有显著优势。2023年，中国数字经济规模已超过55万亿元，数字经济核心产业增加值占GDP的比重达10%左右，充分说明中国与东盟在数字经济领域的合作潜力巨大、前景广阔。2022年，中国与东盟签署了《落实中国—东盟数字经济合作伙伴关系行动计划（2021—2025）》，持续加强在数字经济领域的合作。预计2025年，数字经济将继续成为中国—东盟双向投资的重要领域，双方将在电子商务、金融科技、数字基础设施、智慧城市等方面进一步加强合作，促进双边数字经济投资，实现以数字经济促共同发展的美好愿景。

5. 绿色低碳经济投资前景广阔

据《2022年东南亚绿色经济报告》估算，东盟国家需1万亿至3万亿美元投资以实现2030年碳减排目标，东盟国家的能源需求在2030年前也将增加近50%。与此同时，中国在绿色低碳经济方面拥有丰富的经验和技术优势，在太阳能、风能、核能等领域的技术和产业化能力也处于世界领先地位。2023年，中国的可再生能源装机容量达到12亿千瓦，占全球总量三成以上。此外，中国企业还助推东盟国家提高能源效率、实现节能减排，并于2022年与新加坡联合成立了"中新绿色金融合作示范区"，进一步推动绿色金融领域的合作。预计2025年，中国—东盟在可再生能源、节能减排、绿色金融等方面的合作将进一步深化，为区域经济的可持续发展奠定坚实基础，并为实现全球气候目标贡献重要力量。

（三）服务贸易

RCEP 与中国—东盟 3.0 版谈判的叠加机遇下，中国—东盟自由贸易的主要障碍已经从货物贸易领域内的关税壁垒转向服务贸易与投资领域内的监管、非关税壁垒以及市场的开放度。中国—东盟应进一步加强重点领域合作，深化双向投资，促进服务要素的自由流动，从而推动服务贸易的进一步发展。

1. 服务业重点领域深化改革开放

巩固传统服务部门如旅游、运输、其他商业服务的发展。旅游服务是中国—东盟服务贸易的重要组成部分，虽然新冠疫情对旅游业造成了较大的冲击，但东盟国家有着旅游资源丰富、配套设施较为完善、上下游产业较为完整等优势，在旅游服务出口上具有优势；同时中国的旅游资源具有异质性，且与东盟国家具有相近的文化背景，双方在旅游合作方面具有较大的合作空间。运输服务需求愈加强烈。随着中国以及发达国家产业结构调整，部分产业转移到越南、泰国、印度尼西亚等地区，中国—东盟区域产业链的构建将带动运输、金融等相关服务的发展，运输服务作为中国—东盟合作的传统服务部门，将激发新的增长点和增长潜力，叠加棕榈油、铁矿石、天然气、大米等为代表的大宗产品交易规模持续上升，在带动中国—东盟的大宗商品物流体系建设的同时，运输行业将迎来新发展。

加快新兴服务部门如金融保险、电信、计算机等新兴服务领域的产业合作。金融保险、电信、计算机是中国—东盟合作的重点领域，双边贸易规模迅速增长，但体量仍较小。随着 RCEP、中国—东盟 3.0 版的建设，中国—东盟的金融保险、电信、计算机等将面临更低的市场准入门槛，服务贸易壁垒进一步降低，在区域产业链不断完善、产业布局调整的背景下，金融保险、电信、计算机等将成为区域服务贸易发展的增长极。对电信、金融保险等敏感部门，要进一步扩大开放程度，支持金融、电信的市场化发展，鼓励跨国的合作开发。

2. 探索构建高标准新业态数字经济环境

首先，搭建跨境交流信息共享平台，促进区域内的跨境贸易合作。结合中国—东盟国家特点，与区域内国家的有关部门、研究机构或高校开展合作，建立多语种的服务企业供求信息数据库，将各国投资环境、贸易政策、人才交流、项目供求、融资解决方案等信息分门别类进行共享。其次，建立健全数据共享机制。通过政府间搭建数据共享平台，扩大数据共享范围，发布共享数据目录，搭建数据共享的平台和治理机制，推动构建数字经济国际规则。规范数据跨境流动，构建高标准的数据安全管理认证制度，构建安全、高标准、便利的数据跨境流动新规则，形成区域数据跨境流动的基本规则。

3. 改善规制环境，推进贸易与投资一体化

中国—东盟双方政府要大力发展服务业，优化营商环境，为扩大服务贸易出口提供物质条件。一方面，东盟国家如泰国、越南、印度尼西亚等在继续加强基础设施建设的同时，政府应出台相关扶持政策，吸引更多投资流向东盟，并引导区内外投资更多流向计算机、金融服务、保险及会计、科技服务等新兴服务行业，培育知识密集型服务贸易企业，形成产业集群。另一方面，中国应持续释放政策利好信号，

尽可能地解除对竞争的管制，降低政策的不确定性，简化行政审批手续，降低交易成本，提高企业交易效率，强化市场预期，推动贸易与投资的一体化发展。

4. 推动自然人的跨区域流动

人才培养与技术进步是服务贸易发展的源泉与动力，要积极推动服务贸易人才的培养和人才要素的跨区域流动。在 RCEP 框架下，中国—东盟应进一步降低专业技术人才的流动门槛，逐步完善自然人流动机制，鼓励人才流动。搭建中国—东盟人才跨境流动的平台机制，畅通双方的人才交流，推动人才的跨境流动，进而引进先进的技术和管理经验，促进经验技术和管理经验的交流。人才培养方面，推进国际教育交流合作，推动中国—东盟高校合作，促进高素质人才的跨区域交流，培养国际人才。此外，简化中国—东盟出入境旅游手续，发挥过境免签等政策的作用，激发中国—东盟国的双向旅游，提升旅游便利度，同时加强中国—东盟文化交流，促进双方的文化传播和文化影响力。

（四）中国—东盟自贸区 3.0 版商机前瞻

1. 中国—东盟自贸区 3.0 版对企业的机遇

第一，市场范围扩张，准入机会增加。中国—东盟自贸区是全球覆盖人口最多、发展速度最快的自贸区之一，拥有 19 亿人口的庞大消费市场，企业可以更轻松地进入到这些市场中，吸收新的消费群体，扩张其市场份额。此外，随着贸易便利化水平的提升，企业产品进入区内国家市场的障碍进一步降低，加速了商品在区域内的自由流通。除此之外，自贸区升级还在投资方面创造了更多机会，为企业的长远发展奠定了基础。

第二，降低企业成本，提升企业效益。在产品生产上，通过削减成员国间的关税与非关税壁垒，降低了原材料及中间产品的进口价格，减少了产品生产成本。此外，随着区域内供应链互联互通的深化，企业与上下游产业合作的效率不断提高，资源得到了更高效的利用。在物流与运输成本方面，基础设施建设提升了物流网络的连通性与运作效率，降低了运输总成本。同时，随着贸易便利化水平的提高、制度的透明度与一致性提升，企业的合规成本被进一步压缩。

第三，强化技术合作，增加创新机会。加速与国际经贸规则对接，深化技术经济合作，推动企业技术创新和产业升级。在技术升级方面，引导企业加强研发投入，支持新技术、新工艺和新材料的应用。同时，加快传统产业升级步伐，以数字化、可持续发展为重点，推动形成更高效的产业增长模式。此外，企业可以借助自贸区平台，积极扩展国际合作机会。在知识产权保护方面，通过加强修订相关法规，进行法律国际合作，建立更高效的知识产权保护体系，激发创新活力。

第四，把握新的增长点，实现现代化发展。数字经济和绿色经济代表着未来经济发展的趋势，自贸区的升级为企业在这些领域的发展提供了新的增长点和机遇。首先，数字经济和绿色经济本身就具有庞大的市场空间，消费者对数字化、可持续产品和服务的需求将持续增长。其次，企业还可以将原有业务与数字、绿色相结合，通过数字融合提升决策水平和企业运营效率，通过可持续发展承担社会责任，提升企业的社会形象。

2. 中国—东盟自贸区3.0版对中国的机遇

第一，把握两个市场两种资源，推动双循环格局建设。中国—东盟自贸区 3.0 版的建设不仅意味着中国企业可以更便捷地进入东盟市场，同时也为东盟国家的产品和服务进入中国市场提供更广阔的空间。通过这种双向开放的市场，中国可以更好地利用国内和国际两种资源、两个市场，推动构建新发展格局，建成国内大循环为主体、国内国际双循环相互促进的经济格局。通过深化与东盟国家的经济合作，中国也将更有效地应对外部经济环境的变化，提升经济的韧性和抗风险能力。

第二，加快新旧动能转换，推动经济结构升级。随着中国经济的快速发展，传统的经济增长模式难以适应时代发展，因此，需加快传统产业向高端化、智能化、绿色化方向变革，培育壮大新兴产业，形成新的经济增长点。新兴产业可以凭借自贸区内更多的优惠政策和发展机会，实现快速发展，助力中国经济结构的优化和升级。随着市场的相互开放，新的消费需求被创造，促使中国企业开发适应市场需求的新产品和新服务，推动消费升级和产业结构调整。

第三，增强政治互信，促进区域稳定。中国—东盟自贸区在增强政治互信和促进区域稳定方面扮演着重要角色。自贸区为成员国提供了一个多边交流和合作的平台，定期的磋商和对话机制增进了彼此的信任和了解。此外，随着中国—东盟自贸区的项目数量和人员往来增加，增进了双方人民的友谊，为政治互信打下社会基础。

3. 中国—东盟自贸区 3.0 版对东盟的机遇

第一，加快经济发展，提升社会福祉。首先，自贸区为东盟国家的特色产品进一步打开了中国市场，为东盟国家带来了显著的出口增长和外汇收入。其次，自贸区框架下，东盟国家积极吸引国际投资，加速了经济结构的转型升级。在此基础上，产生了大量就业机会，随着就业率和收入的增加，贫困人口的规模进一步下降，社会整体福祉水平显著提升。

第二，加快基础设施建设，实现互联互通。自贸区能够为东盟国家带来更多的资金支持以及丰富经验，通过基础设施建设，加快区域互联互通。更高效的运输和物流网络将促进区域内资源的自由流动，有效降低了交易成本，为区域内企业提供了更加灵活、更具韧性的供应链，整体运营效率有望进一步提升。此外，互联互通的增强在提升经济效率的同时，也通过更可靠的交通设施、更高效的沟通网络增强了国民获取更公平社会资源的可能性。

第三，加快技能与知识转移。中国—东盟自贸区3.0版的建设不仅为东盟国家带来了经济利益，还促进了技能与知识的有效转移。在自贸区框架下，东盟国家可以更容易地从中国引进先进的生产技术和经验。在教育合作方面，东盟国家积极增强与中国院校的交流合作，提高东盟学生在中国的学习机会。通过这些措施，东盟国家还能根据自身实际情况进行因地制宜的适应和调整，以实现更有效的社会发展和经济增长。

4. 中国—东盟自贸区3.0版的经贸潜力

第一，东盟经济水平持续提升。如图8所示，自2013年以来，东盟的GDP始终呈现出稳定的增长趋势，从2.51万亿美元增长至2022年的3.62万亿美元。这种增长展示了东盟在全球经济中的竞争力，也展现了东盟市场对外部投资者的吸引力。特别是在2017年和2022年，GDP增长率分别达到了5.4%和5.6%，显示出强劲的经济增长势头。东盟经济体还展现出了强大的韧性。特别是2020年经历了短期的经济衰退后，次年就迅速回升，GDP总量超过下降前一年水平，这表明东盟国家有能力采取有效的政策措施来应对经济不确定的挑战。

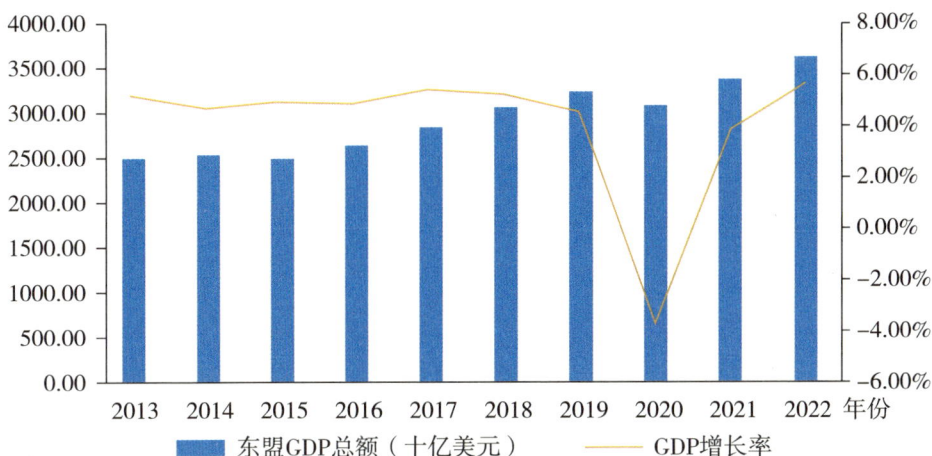

图 8　东盟 GDP 总额与增长率

数据来源：*ASEAN STATISTICAL YEARBOOK 2023*。

　　第二，东盟人口稳定增长，收入持续提高。如图 9 所示，2013—2022 年，东盟的人口从 6.12 亿增长到 6.71 亿人，年增长率保持在 1% 左右，劳动力市场和消费市场逐年扩大。人口的增长为中国企业提供了更广阔的市场空间，尤其是在基本生活需求和服务业领域。东盟人均 GDP 从 2013 年的 4105.20 美元增长到 2022 年的 5391.80 美元，随着居民收入水平的提高和消费升级，消费者对高质量商品和服务的需求增加。两个因素相互作用，共同推动了中国与东盟之间的经贸合作和区域经济一体化进程。

　　第三，产业结构不断优化。如图 10 所示，制造业在东盟经济中占有最高的比重，达到 21.20%。随着中国制造业的升级，一些劳动密集型和资源密集型产业正在向东盟转移，这不仅为东盟带来了就业机会和技术转让，也为中国企业家提供了新的投资热点和市场空间。金融和保险、信息与通信以及公共行政和其他服务活动也是东盟经济的重要组成部分，分别占 6.70%、4% 和 10.30%。这些领域为双方提供了合作的机会，特别是在金融科技、数字化建设和基础设施投资等方面。

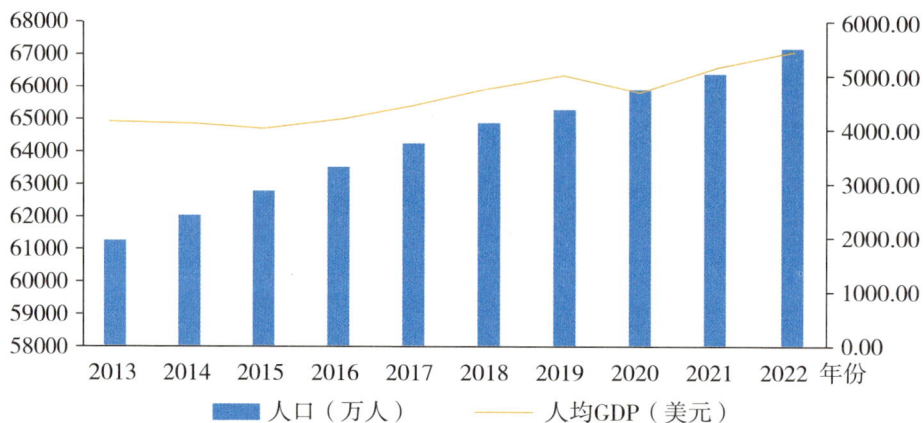

图 9　东盟人口总数与人均 GDP

数据来源：*ASEAN STATISTICAL YEARBOOK 2023*。

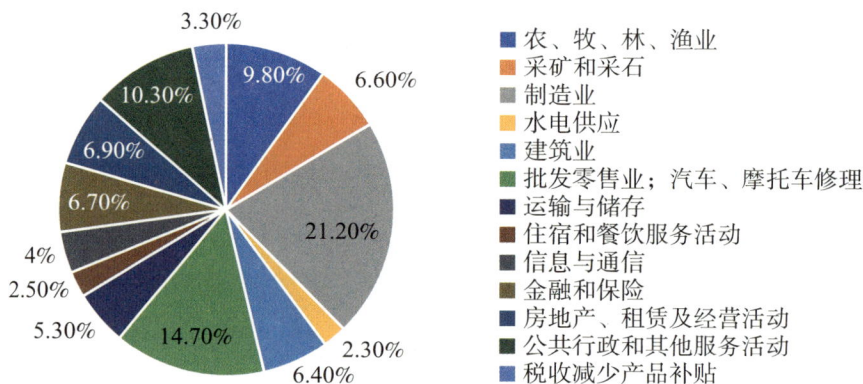

图 10　2022 年东盟各产业份额

数据来源：*ASEAN STATISTICAL YEARBOOK 2023*。

第四，中国—东盟贸易水平较高。自中国—东盟自贸区成立以来，双方经贸往来快速发展，随着 RCEP 生效、西部陆海新通道建设等政策红利持续释放，双边贸易规模进一步扩大。2010—2023 年，中国—东盟贸易额总体呈增长趋势，双边贸易额从 2928 亿美元增长到 9117 亿美元，年均增长 11.54%，中国与东盟互为最大贸易伙伴的地位在一段时间内不会发生改变（见表 8）。

表 8　2010—2023 年中国—东盟贸易额、增速与其占中国对外贸易比重

年份	中国—东盟贸易额 （亿美元）	增速 （%）	中国—东盟贸易占中国贸易比重 （%）
2010	2928	37.5	9.85
2011	3628.5	24	9.96
2012	4000.9	10.2	10.35
2013	4436	10.9	10.67
2014	4804	8.3	11.17
2015	4721.6	−1.7	11.94
2016	4522	−4.2	12.27
2017	5148	13.8	12.53
2018	5878.7	14.1	12.72
2019	6414.6	9.2	14.01
2020	6846	6.7	14.70
2021	8782	28.1	14.65
2022	9753.4	11.2	15.56
2023	9117	−6.5	15.36

数据来源：根据 UN Comtrade、中国国家统计局数据库数据整理得出。

5. 专家视角：中国—东盟自贸区 3.0 版突破方向

第一，持续优化贸易投资水平。中国—东盟自贸区 3.0 有望实现

更多的商品零关税的同时，简化通关手续加强统一标准建设，通过建立统一的商品检验标准，减少非关税壁垒，提高贸易便利化水平。在服务贸易领域，加快以数字贸易为主导的服务贸易供给侧结构优化升级，探索建立更高效的服务贸易管理新模式，完善服务行业开放的风险防控体系。在投资领域，进一步优化区域投资结构和产业布局升级，促进高科技和高附加值产业的直接投资，而且向国际社会发送积极信号，增强外资企业对中国—东盟市场的信心。

第二，加强数字经济合作。通过自贸区 3.0 版合作，提升区内国家数字化水平，缩小区域内的数字鸿沟，推动成员国共享成果。中国与东盟在与数字经济发展领域达成一致意见并签署合作协议，发挥政策高地的原动力作用，在加强数字经济基础设施合作的基础上，通过加快技术交流和知识共享，构建更高效、透明和智能化供应链，加快数字化人才培养，缩小双方在数字经济上的差距，为合作打下良好基础。

第三，加快绿色可持续发展。中国—东盟自贸区 3.0 版的建设，不仅是对过往合作成果的深化与拓展，更是双方共同应对全球气候变化挑战、推动绿色低碳转型的重要一环。随着双方绿色经济合作的深入发展，绿色产业机会不断扩展、发展空间持续增加，将建成一个覆盖更广、层次更深的绿色经济市场。中国东盟双方将不断加强政策协调和法规整合，共同制定绿色经济合作标准，以促进跨境环境管理的有效性和资源利用的可持续性，为全球绿色经济治理体系贡献力量。

第四，推动智慧城市建设，激发经济潜力。中国—东盟合作还激发了城市的经济潜力，提升了城市的竞争力，城市应抓住这一机遇，加强"智慧城市"建设，提升治理能力和服务水平，从城市基础设施建设和公共服务领域入手，加快数字经济与城市发展的深度融合，打破地域限制促进资源共享，实现可持续发展。

第五，推动"10+1+1"扩展，提升整体福利水平。加快 RCEP 在东盟范围内的生效进程，就启动中国—东盟自贸区 3.0 版的谈判达成一致意见，按照既定程序启动建设。中国—东盟自贸区 3.0 版能增强自贸区的贸易扩大效应、贸易转移效应、贸易创造效应等，增加中国与东盟的整体福利水平。

第六，加快区域经济合作，提高区域一体化水平。中国东盟双方在硬件联通的基础上，还关注加强制度规则对接、人文交流等软联通的密切程度，以提升双方之间的互信与合作。此外，中国与东盟双方可以利用各自的独特优势，形成强有力的合作互补效应，通过整合优势资源提高国际市场竞争力，共同寻找并开发具有潜力的第三方市场。

四、中国—东盟经贸合作新亮点

（一）明星行业

1. 第一产业的明星行业——现代水果产业

（1）合作背景与基础

共建"一带一路"倡议和《区域全面经济伙伴关系协定》（RCEP）为中国和东盟水果领域经贸合作奠定了坚实基础。中国各地特色水果正通过政策桥梁，远销至与中国地理相邻、水果品种互补的东盟国家；同时，东盟国家丰富的热带水果资源也正大量进入中国市场。

水果加工为中国与东盟果业的双向奔赴增添了更多色彩。现代水果产业的发展使中国—东盟水果贸易超越了单纯的生鲜交易范畴，向着高附加值的产业链上下游延伸，形成了从种植、采摘到初加工、深加工的完整产业链。

（2）市场数据与表现

中国与东盟间水果贸易往来紧密联系。泰国、越南、菲律宾和印尼是中国水果的主要贸易国。据联合国贸易数据库统计，2013—2022年间，中国对其水果贸易额分别增长了224%、103%、101%和70%，增长势头强劲。^① 结合图 11 可知，中国从东盟的水果进口逐年攀升，2023 年增长了 32.3%；中国出口至东盟的水果虽有所下降，但降幅不大且金额相对较小，且进出口总额呈上涨态势。

単位：亿元/人民币

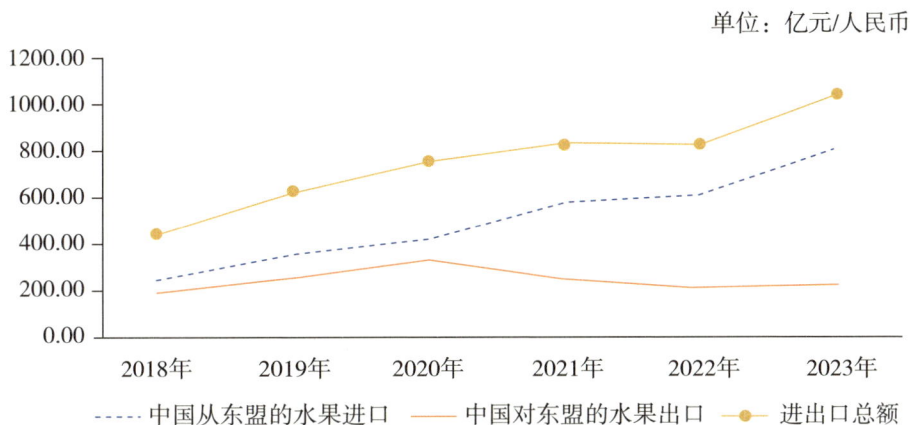

图 11 中国与东盟国家的水果进出口额

数据来源：根据中国海关总署数据整理得出。

注：水果 HS 编码使用 08-食用水果及坚果、甜瓜或柑橘属水果的果皮统计得出。

深加工、高附加值等水果产业转型升级构筑了中国—东盟现代水果产业合作的底色。广西壮族自治区亚热带作物研究所等单位首创原果风味果脯加工技术，带动国际原果风味果脯加工产业的发展，构建了中国—东盟及非洲原果风味果脯加工产业集群，年产值达 50 亿元；凭祥产业园引进了盐津铺子、生和堂等农副产品加工企业，形成了东

---

① 中国—东盟传媒网.“一带一路”：中国—东盟的瓜果飘香之路［EB/OL］.（2024-07-02）［2024-07-28］. https://www.sohu.com/a/790184082_402008.

盟特色产品深加工跨境产业链①。结合图 12 可见，中国与东盟水果制成品贸易不断深化，反映出中国和东盟国家水果制成品贸易的强大潜力，2023 年中国自东盟的水果制成品进口增幅高达 37.9%。

单位：亿元/人民币

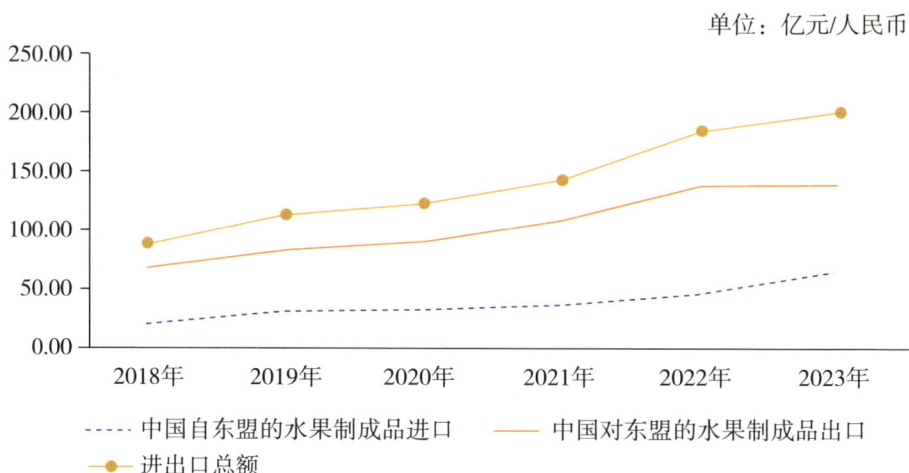

图 12　中国与东盟国家的水果制成品进出口额

数据来源：根据中国海关总署数据整理得出。

注：水果等制成品 HS 编码使用 20-蔬菜、水果、坚果或植物其他部分的制品统计得出。

（3）合作成果与突破

一是 RCEP 为中国—东盟水果产业发展注入新动能。 RCEP 通过降低关税、简化海关程序，减少了水果这类易腐商品的滞港时间，同时原产地规则更为灵活，有助于利用区域内资源进行深加工；RCEP 生效实施以来，东盟国家新获准入中国市场的水果品种已包括柬埔寨龙眼、

① 钟金炽. 崇左：助力实现"东盟水果自由"［N/OL］. 左江日报，2024-07-14［2024-07-28］. http://szb.gxcznews.com.cn:8088/pc/content/202407/14/content_58773.html.

越南榴莲等 8 种；截至目前，东盟已有 20 多种新鲜水果获得准入。①
2023 年 4 月，马来西亚成为继泰国和越南之后获准对中国出口菠萝蜜
的第三个国家。②

二是产业深加工赋能水果产业纵深发展。中国—东盟（崇左）水
果交易中心核心区主要建设有展示推广、产品集散、线上交易、智慧
物流、查验通关、电子商务以及落地加工等功能；加工区以落地加工、
冷链仓储功能为主，打造面向东盟及全国的水果加工产业集群，发展
落地加工、精深加工等业务。③

（4）未来趋势与展望

**一是充分发挥 RCEP、中国—东盟自贸区（CAFTA）等协定的贸
易创造效应。**其一，进一步放宽双边水果市场准入，减少或取消关税
壁垒，使得更多的水果品种能够顺利进入市场。其二，拓展水果可贸
易种类。通过协商调整原产地规则等方式，允许更多种类水果被列入
可贸易清单。其三，进一步拓展贸易伙伴。除了与中国已有紧密往来
的泰国、越南、菲律宾和印度尼西亚外，还可以进一步拓展与新加坡
等东盟国家的合作。

二是全面推动水果贸易向更深层次、更广阔领域发展。延伸产业
链、深挖产品附加值已成为初级农产品转型升级、拓宽国际市场、

---

① 罗婧. RCEP 政策红利持续释放东南亚水果在广西"抢鲜"进境［N/OL］.
广西日报，2023－06－29［2024－07－28］. https://gxrb.gxrb.com.cn/?name＝gxrb&date＝
2023－06－29&code＝001&xuhao＝8.

② 刘旭. 甜蜜有加的中马农业合作［N/OL］. 国际商报，2024－04－22［2024－
07－28］. https://epa.comnews.cn/pc/content/202404/22/content_15429.html.

③ 廖法丽. 鲜果满园幸福来——我市推动水果产业高质量发展综述［N/OL］.
左江日报，2024－02－18［2024－07－28］. http://szb.gxcznews.com.cn:8088/pc/content/
202402/18/content_53679.html.

提升贸易效益的关键路径。智慧果园与设施果业的兴起，正引领着水果产业的新一轮革命。通过引入物联网、大数据、人工智能等现代信息技术，可以实现精准灌溉、病虫害智能预警等先进种植技术的应用。

2. 第二产业的明星行业——高端装备制造业

（1）合作背景与基础

产业升级的发展愿景与诉求构成了中国和东盟国家在高端装备制造业深入合作的坚实基础。 中国的高端装备制造业面临着国际技术壁垒和市场竞争的严峻考验。东盟作为中国在这一战略性新兴产业中不可或缺的贸易伙伴，凭借其独特的地理位置、丰富的资源禀赋以及日益紧密的区域经济合作机制，成为中国高端装备制造业寻求新增长点、拓展合作版图的重要支撑。

在电力装备制造领域，中国生产的电力产品、从事的电力工程项目、电力设计项目的性价比优势明显，符合东盟国家庞大的电力需求。 中国—东盟在电力行业已有良好的基础，如《澜沧江—湄公河合作五年行动计划（2023—2027）》提出，加强各国电力规划沟通，共同促进区域电网建设、改造和重建。[①] **轨道交通装备制造领域同样展现出广阔的合作前景。** 中国拥有完善的轨道交通产业链和先进的制造技术，而东盟国家则处于快速工业化和城市化进程中，对轨道交通装备的需求日益增长。**在清洁装备制造领域，随着全球能源转型和气候变化挑战的加剧，这一领域成为推动双方经济绿色发展的重要方向。** 面临能

---

① 中国政府网. 澜沧江—湄公河合作五年行动计划（2023—2027）［EB/OL］.（2023-12-26）［2024-07-28］. https://www.gov.cn/yaowen/liebiao/202312/content_6922341.htm.

源结构转型的压力，清洁能源装备作为实现能源转型的关键，其制造和应用对于双方来说都具有重要意义。

（2）市场数据与表现

据中国海关总署数据，在 2010—2020 年间，中国对东盟国家出口高端装备制造产品贸易总额由 299.55 亿美元增长至 1119.04 亿美元，贸易额年均增长率为 12.73%[①]。2023 年重庆市涪陵区对东盟国家的机电产品出口金额达 4.2 亿元，同比增长 140%[②]。中国企业在东盟国家的海上风电项目成果丰硕，中国企业已在越南承建了金瓯 350 兆瓦海上风电、朔庄薄寮 171 兆瓦海上风电、平大 310 兆瓦海上风电等项目。此外，中国远景能源集团还将作为合作方之一，为位于泰国湾的 Hanuman260 兆瓦风电项目提供 65 台 4 兆瓦海上风电机组[③]。2023 年 9 月，由中车株洲所自主研发制造的新型绿色轨道交通工具——全球首辆氢能源智轨电车正式亮相马来西亚[④]。结合图 13 分析可知，虽然 2023 年中国—东盟高端装备制造贸易往来略有下降，但其自 2018 年起高速增长，2023 年间中国自东盟的高端装备进口是 2018 年的 1.25 倍，对东盟的出口是 2018 年的 1.76 倍。

---

① 乐为，陈佳. 高端装备制造业贸易强度如何影响出口技术复杂度？——基于中国—东盟样本数据的分析 [J]. 对外经贸实务，2024，42（4）：17-25.

② 中国新闻网. 重庆加强与东盟国家贸易合作聚焦电力装备制造业 [EB/OL]. （2024－06－18）[2024－07－28]. https://www.chinanews.com.cn/cj/2024/06－18/10236262.shtml.

③ 东博社. RCEP 开辟中国—东盟海上风电合作新空间 [EB/OL]. （2023－09－12）[2024－07－28]. https://baijiahao.baidu.com/s?id=1776843883370182214.

④ 人民网—国际频道. 全球首列氢能源智轨电车在马来西亚正式试跑 [EB/OL]. （2023－09－07）[2024－07－28]. http://world.people.com.cn/n1/2023/0907/c1002-40072689.html.

单位：亿元/人民币

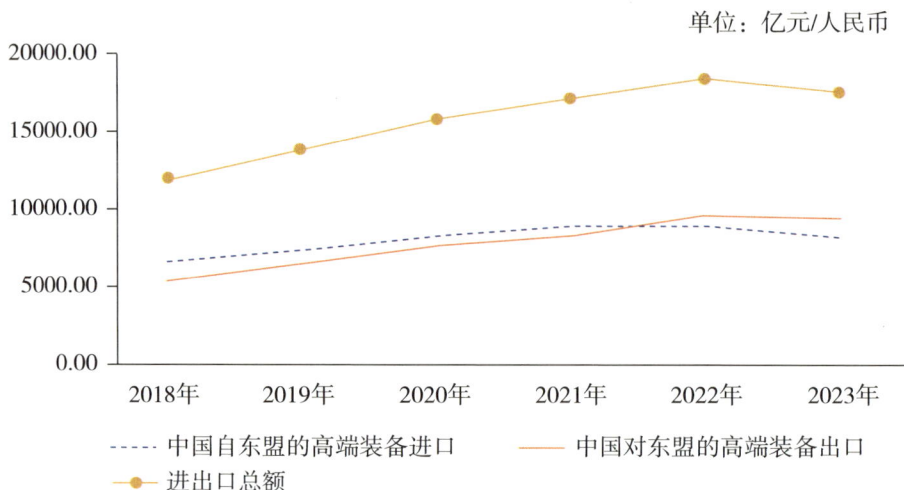

图 13　中国与东盟国家的高端装备制造进出口额

数据来源：根据中国海关总署数据整理得出。

注：高端装备制造使用 HS 编码中的 85-电机、电气设备及其零件；录音机及放声机、电视图像、声音的录制和重放设备及其零件、附件；86-铁道及电车道机车、车辆及其零件；铁道及电车道轨道固定装置及其零件；附件；各种机械（包括电动机械）交通信号设备；88-航空器、航天器及其零件；89-船舶及浮动结构体等统计得出。

（3）合作成果与突破

一是装备制造产业合作论坛为中国—东盟在高端装备制造领域发展提供新机遇。2023 年中国（广西）—东盟应急装备和技术展在广西南宁市隆重举行，集中展示了应急救援领域的高端装备和技术。[①] 同年"中国—东盟清洁能源合作中心"取得了显著进展，通过举办清洁能源合作周、东盟海上风电+示范项目潜力专题会议等活动，搭建了

---

① 广西网络广播电视台. 2023 年中国（广西）—东盟应急装备和技术展在南宁举办［EB/OL］.（2023－12－07）［2024－07－28］. https://news.gxtv.cn/article/detail_c5e272c97f7a4f02a648d96693790b56.html.

广泛的交流平台。① 此外，2023 年中国—东盟制造业与职业教育合作发展论坛，搭建了中国—东盟智能制造人才培养新平台，推动成为未来制造业"智能化、网络化、绿色化"新高地。②

二是绿色低碳项目成为中国—东盟高端装备制造经贸合作的新亮点。 国家能源局局长章建华在 2023 中国—东盟清洁能源合作周开幕式上指出，未来，中方愿与东盟国家继续加强区域互联互通、可再生能源、能力建设和绿色投资等方面务实合作，积极推动中国—东盟清洁能源合作中心成立。在第 20 届中国—东盟博览会上，绿色化工新材料、高端金属新材料等新兴产业项目占比达 78%，其中海上风电、光伏储能等绿色低碳项目数量和投资总额占大会集中签约项目的近四成。③

（4）未来趋势与展望

一是深入拓展重点领域高端装备制造的合作往来。加强在风电、光伏、水电等清洁能源装备的研发、制造和应用方面的合作；加强在智能制造装备、工业机器人线等领域的合作；进一步深化在航空航天技术研发、生产制造、市场开拓等方面的合作。随着东盟国家基础设施建设的不断推进、轨道交通装备需求持续增长，双方在轨道交通装

---

① 国家能源局. 2023 中国—东盟清洁能源合作周在海口市开幕［EB/OL］.（2023－09－20）［2024－07－28］. https://www.nea.gov.cn/2023－09/20/c_1310742167.htm.

② 人民网—广西频道. 2023 中国—东盟制造业与职业教育合作发展论坛在南宁举行［EB/OL］.（2023－09－17）［2024－07－28］. http://gx.people.com.cn/n2/2023/0917/c179464-40573874.html.

③ 中国新闻网. 第 20 届东博会签约总投资 4873 亿元投资总额创历届新高［EB/OL］.（2023－09－18）［2024－07－28］. https://www.chinanews.com.cn/cj/2023/09－18/10079708.shtml.

备研发、制造、运营和维护等方面的合作需求亟待进一步挖掘释放。

二是依托产业园区释放高端装备制造发展潜力。依托两国双园、高端装备制造产业园区等，实现从原材料采购、零部件制造到整机组装、物流配送的全链条优化，通过信息共享、资源互补，有效降低生产成本、提高生产效率，进而增强高端装备制造产业链的韧性和稳定性。

3. 第二产业的明星行业——新能源网联汽车

（1）合作背景与基础

中国与东盟在新能源网联汽车领域的供需基础为其发展提供可能。中国在新能源网联汽车树立了鲜明的"领跑者"形象；东盟国家作为新兴市场，对新能源汽车的需求呈现出井喷态势。随着环保意识的提升和能源结构的转型，东盟国家政府正积极出台各项政策措施，鼓励新能源汽车的普及与应用。

基于产业链、价值链的深入合作拓展了中国与东盟在新能源网联汽车领域的合作利益。中国电机与电控系统等新能源网联技术的智能化、集成化发展，进一步提升了车辆的动力性能和操控精准度。与此同时，东盟国家在原材料供应和零部件生产方面展现出显著优势。

（2）市场数据与表现

根据中国海关数据显示，2023年我国对东盟出口新能源汽车32万辆、同比增长98%，出口量占我国新能源汽车全部出口量的18%。2023年中国品牌占东盟新能源汽车销量的比例达67%，其中比亚迪、上汽名爵、哪吒位居销量前三位，合计市场份额超过50%。[①] 据泰国

---

① 数字经济创新联合实验室. 深化与东盟新能源汽车产业合作的机遇、挑战和建议［EB/OL］.（2024－07－03）［2024－07－28］. https://www.163.com/dy/article/J66AJCC50553BGD2.html.

汽车协会统计，2023 年泰国电动汽车总登记量约 7.6 万辆，占汽车登记总量的 12%，其中前四名均为中国品牌，前十名内中国品牌占 8 个席位。① 根据图 14 可知，2021 年中国与东盟的新能源汽车贸易处于起步阶段，近年来中国对东盟国家新能源汽车出口金额呈现明显上升态势，2022 年上涨幅度达 250.04%，2023 年上涨幅度高达 367.49%。

单位：亿元/人民币

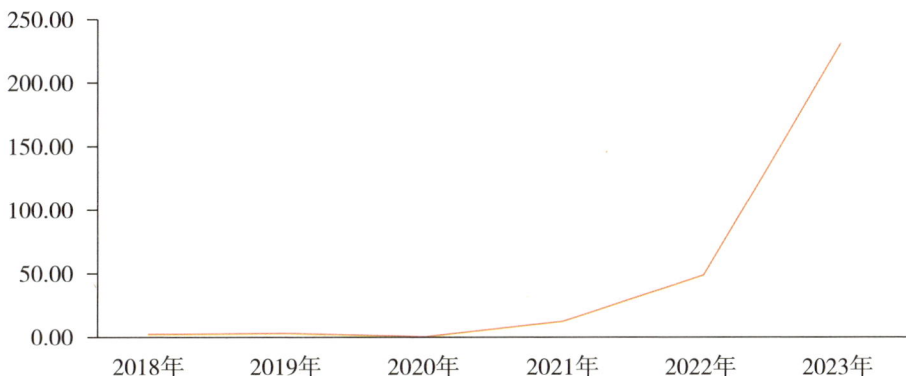

图 14　中国对东盟国家的新能源汽车出口额

数据来源：根据中国海关总署数据整理得出。

注：新能源汽车行业进出口贸易统计使用 HS 编码中的 870340、870350、870360、870380 统计得出。

（3）合作成果与突破

一是中国在东盟的新能源汽车投资布局取得深入进展。上汽、长城在泰国等国建有整车工厂，长安、比亚迪泰国工厂开工建设，广汽、

---

① 新华网. 记者手记｜中国电动汽车"给泰国消费者带来惊喜"［EB/OL］. （2024-07-22）［2024-07-28］. http://www.news.cn/fortune/20240722/a8a4d8da31b9482980b53099586f271e/c.html.

奇瑞等企业拟在东盟投资建厂，宁德时代等动力电池企业、华友钴业等材料企业、华域汽车等零部件企业也在东盟投资布局。

二是技术知识开辟中国—东盟汽车产业合作新时代。上汽通用五菱帮助东盟建立新能源汽车核心技术和生态标准，实现了产品和标准的双向输出。依托 GSEV 等新能源产品与东盟市场的高契合度，因地制宜选择合作模式，成功出口印度尼西亚、越南、泰国、老挝、缅甸、柬埔寨等东盟国家。[①]

（4）未来趋势与展望

一是进一步深化技术交流与合作。其一是加强核心技术联合研发。通过共享研究成果、联合设立研发中心等方式，共同攻克自动驾驶技术中关键难题，构建更加安全、高效、便捷的智能交通网络。其二是随着中国—东盟新能源汽车检测认证联盟的成立与发展，应加快推动新能源汽车技术标准的互认进程。

二是进一步鼓励双方企业加速出海。鼓励通过合资建厂、技术合作等多元化方式，实现优势互补与资源共享。同时，企业自身也应积极行动，主动与东盟本地的产业链企业、行业组织等建立紧密的战略合作关系。通过加强沟通与协作，共同探索市场潜力。

4. 第三产业的明星行业——现代运输业

（1）合作背景与基础

深厚的政策合作基础对中国—东盟的现代运输业发展提出了广泛需求。中国与东盟国家在基础设施建设取得了显著成就，为现代运输

---

① 中国质量万里行促进会. 中国质量万里行·典型丝路品牌 | 上汽通用五菱：打造"一带一路"新能源产业合作典范 共创高质量发展 ［EB/OL］. （2023–12–15）［2024–07–29］. https://www.caqp.org.cn/hy/qyfc/1091.html.

业的发展铺设了紧密合作的桥梁。中国与东盟国家在经贸领域的合作日益紧密，贸易额与投资规模持续攀升，在这一背景下，加强现代运输业的合作显得尤为重要。

交通网络的互联互通为中国与东盟现代运输业的发展提供了坚实的物质基础。中国与东盟共同实施铁路、公路、港口等基础设施项目，实现了交通网络的互联互通。西部陆海新通道承担着中国西部内陆腹地通达东盟、连接世界的桥梁和枢纽的重任。此外，泛亚铁路网、昆明—曼谷高速公路、马来西亚关丹港、印尼雅加达丹戎不碌港等，极大的提高了货物处理能力和物流效率。

（2）市场数据与表现

2022 年，我国以铁路、水路、航空运输方式对东盟进出口分别增长了 197.6%、26.7% 和 15.5%。2021 年底中老铁路建成通车；2022 年，我国与东盟通过铁路运输货物中，经过中老铁路运输的比重跃升到 44.7%，对中国与东盟之间以铁路运输方式进出口增长贡献率超过 60%；[①] 2023 年，通过西部陆海新通道运输的集装箱货物达到 86.1 万标箱，较 2017 年的 3382 标箱激增 254 倍，充分体现了新通道高效便捷的物流优势。[②] 根据表 9 可知，西部陆海新通道的国际铁路联运班列，全程采用铁路运输方式，通过广西凭祥、云南磨憨等口岸出境至越南、老挝等东盟国家，其运输数据展现了中国和东盟现代运输业的

① 海关发布. 国新办发布会｜2022 年我国外贸规模再创历史新高［EB/OL］.（2023 – 01 – 12）［2024 – 07 – 29］. https：//baijiahao. baidu. com/s? id = 1754907547729769989.

② 周仕兴，王瑾雯. 西部陆海新通道跑出"加速度"［N/OL］. 光明日报，2024-07-16［2024 – 07 – 29］. https：//epaper. gmw. cn/gmrb/html/2024 – 07/16/nw. D110000gmrb_20240716_2-04. htm.

高速发展。

表9　2021—2023年西部陆海新通道国际铁路联运班列情况

西部陆海新通道国际铁路联运班列	2021 年	2022 年	2023 年
开行列数（列、车次）	—	820	827
运输箱量（标箱）	12050	20002	13854
运输货值（亿元）	28.5	43.8	33.7
开行列数同比增幅（%）	—	90	34
运输箱量同比增幅（%）	131.7	66	−17
运输货值同比增幅（%）	−25	51	−3

数据来源：根据西部陆海新通道门户网整理得出。

（3）合作成果与突破

一是冷链运输等现代运输业新业态不断展现。中老泰冷链班列通过汽车运输进入老挝后，经中老铁路直达重庆小南垭站，全程（泰国果园—重庆小南垭）运行88小时，其中，从老挝万象南站到重庆小南垭站铁路运行仅52小时，相较传统的海运和陆运路线，时间更短、成本更低、运输更加高效。①

二是中国—东盟多式联运取得新进展。中国—东盟多式联运联盟是由中新南宁国际物流园倡议并发起成立的国际性行业组织。联盟的宗旨是依托国际陆海新通道建设，推动中国与东盟乃至中亚及亚太区域其他国家之间的经贸、物流、产能、人文交流等多领域的合作与发

---

① 刘丽靓. 从10天到4天榴莲快车展现通道经济"加速度"[N/OL]. 光明日报，2023-06-13［2024-07-29］. https://www.cs.com.cn/xwzx/hg/202306/t20230613_6349798.html.

展。① 已形成北部湾港海铁联运班列、中越跨境班列等多种物流组织模式。

（4）未来趋势与展望

一是进一步丰富运输业发展的物质基础。随着中老铁路的成功运营，可以建设或扩建更多的铁路线路；继续推进跨国公路和桥梁的建设，进一步提高道路运输的连通性和效率；加大对现有港口的升级改造力度，提高货物吞吐能力，并可能新建更多的现代化港口。

二是推进运输业绿色化、智能化发展。绿色化方面要在公路运输方面推广使用电动汽车、氢能车等新能源交通工具，减少化石燃料消耗和温室气体排放，鼓励优先选择低碳排放的运输方式；智能化方面可以构建完善的跨境综合交通信息化体系，建设多式联运运输一体化综合运行智能监测中心，发展智能物流系统，利用人工智能、大数据等技术优化路线规划、库存管理等，如引入机器人技术进行自动拣选、包装和装载，提高仓库作业效率。

（二）明星企业

明星企业指的是那些在中国与东盟经贸合作中扮演关键角色，具有显著市场影响力、技术创新能力和品牌知名度的企业。需要说明的是，本报告所列举的明星企业，仅是这些杰出典范中的一部分代表性企业，他们以其独特的行业贡献、创新能力以及市场影响力，生动展现了中国与东盟经贸合作的广度和深度。这些企业不仅推动了经贸合作的深化，还引领了相关行业的发展方向。

---

① 中国—东盟多式联运联盟［2024-07-29］．https://www.gcamta.com/channels/2.html.

1. 鑫荣懋果业科技集团

鑫荣懋果业科技集团是一家长期聚焦于水果领域的龙头企业，链接全球核心水果资源，与泰国、智利、新西兰、菲律宾、秘鲁、越南等20多个共建"一带一路"国家紧密合作，集团水果年交易量可达20多万吨。[①] 其中，榴莲是鑫荣懋集团与东盟国家交易的优势特色产品。自2003年起，鑫荣懋集团便开始布局榴莲产业链，打造了全国高端榴莲销量第一的"顶榴"品牌——佳沃。

2015年，鑫荣懋集团在泰国当地投资建设了最大的榴莲加工厂之一——泰果冠集团有限公司，深深植入泰国市场。2024年3月24日，泰国副总理普坦·威乍耶猜对鑫荣懋集团在中泰果业合作中创造佳绩、树立了中泰果业合作典范，给予高度肯定与赞扬，并现场品尝佳沃榴莲、佳沃蓝莓及佳沃易开椰，指出佳沃作为中国的高端水果品牌，亦深受泰国市场欢迎。[②]

2019年马来西亚冷冻榴莲获准入华，鑫荣懋集团作为首批进口商，率先深入马来西亚产区，加速推进马来西亚榴莲进入中国市场的进程，成为马来西亚鲜食榴莲首次登陆中国市场的积极推动者和行业引领者。2024年是中马两国建交50周年暨"中马友好年"，马来西亚鲜食榴莲大门的打开，中国—东盟经贸中的水果产业得到进一步发展，共同促进水果贸易新篇章。

---

① 21世纪经济报道. 专访鑫荣懋集团国际采购平台总经理慕雪平：共建"一带一路"推动果业贸易拓展，加强供应链合作是"必选项"［EB/OL］.（2024-06-28）［2024-07-29］. https://www.21jingji.com/article/20240628/herald/e29efd5cdaec8df127e806f546a3a6c5.html.

② 荣懋企业官网——新鲜水果专家［2024-07-29］. http://joywingmau.com/home/index/index.html.

2. 德尔蒙太平洋有限公司

德尔蒙太平洋有限公司（Del Monte Pacific Limited）是一家全球知名的食品及饮料公司，旗下有 Del Monte、S&W、Contadina 和 College Inn 四个子品牌。整个集团产品涵盖水果罐头、新鲜水果、即食食品等多个品类。

据中国海关总署数据，2023 年中国菠萝进口业务中，对菲律宾的菠萝进口在整个东盟排名第一，年进口金额约 1.8 亿美元，进口量约为 21 万吨。作为菲律宾菠萝业务的巨头，德尔蒙旗下 S&W 早在 2013 年便与中国"佳农"公司结识，并于 2015 年开始合作，双方就大力发展黑钻菠萝产品达成共识，此后一直保持着深度合作关系。[①] 除此之外，为了打开中国市场，S&W 专门为中国市场研制一款菠萝汁，目前该商品在京东、淘宝平台等均有售。

德尔蒙太平洋有限公司除了在中国市场留下战略足迹外，与其他东盟国家也有很紧密的合作关系，其子公司 DMPI 与越南领先的乳制品公司 Vinamilk 于 2021 年 8 月宣布建立战略联盟。[②]

无论是与中国的果业公司合作，还是与越南乳制品公司形成战略联盟，这都是德尔蒙太平洋有限公司打入东盟市场的重要战略。毫无疑问也促进中国—东盟经贸合作全面开花。

3. 中国能源建设股份有限公司

中国能源建设股份有限公司（中国能建）是一家为中国乃至全球

---

① 佳农集团. 叙过往，展新章｜S&W 团队莅临佳农集团［EB/OL］.（2023-03-20）［2024-07-30］. https://www.goodfarmer.com/news/info/93.html.

② 越南通讯社网. 越南乳制品股份公司与菲律宾德尔蒙太平洋建立战略联盟［EB/OL］.（2021-08-17）［2024-07-30］. https://zh.vietnamplus.vn/越南乳制品股份公司与菲律宾德尔蒙太平洋建立战略联盟-post144358.vnp.

能源电力、基础设施等行业提供系统性、一体化、全周期、一揽子发展方案和服务的综合性特大型集团公司。①

2022年8月，中国能建与东博会首次牵手，荣膺第19届东博会首席战略合作伙伴。在第19届中国—东盟博览会期间，中国能建与马来西亚、越南、印度尼西亚、菲律宾等四国连签7单，合同总金额约合人民币135亿元②，为推动促进数智转型、绿色低碳融合发展，服务构建中国—东盟命运共同体，高质量共建"一带一路"提出能建主张，贡献能建方案。中国能建党委书记、董事长宋海良指出，能建新理念新思想新战略在海外逐步落地实践，东南亚作为公司国际业务发展的核心主战场和重要战略市场，要实现东南亚市场的高质量发展，关键在于全力做到"稳增长""强统筹""促转型""广合作""强队伍"上加速领跑。③

中国能建发挥规划、策划引领优势，深化东盟国家新能源交流合作，在老挝牵头完成国家电力规划，签约了老挝装机容量最大/东盟最大单体容量的清洁能源项目——老挝北部互联互通清洁能源基地1.3GW光伏项目；在越南向总理府提交了《越南能源电力业务的合作建议》，和能源院组织专班对接，探索煤电技改、电网升级改造等领域合作路径；在菲律宾组织海上风电等专业论坛，培育海上风电市场，推介中国能建品牌。

---

① 中国能源建设集团有限公司官网［2024-08-10］. https://www.ceec.net.cn/col/col52617/index.html.

② 澎湃新闻. 东博会上，中国能建海外项目七连签，总金额135亿！［EB/OL］.（2022-09-19）［2024-08-10］. https://m.thepaper.cn/baijiahao_19974419.

③ 中国能建新闻中心. 中国能建召开东南亚市场专题会［EB/OL］.（2024-03-24）［2024-08-10］. https://www.ceec.net.cn/art/2024/3/24/art_11016_2530887.html.

截至 2023 年末，中国能建在东盟国家已累计完成投资金额约 140 亿元。投资建设了迄今中国公司在越南单笔投资金额最大的项目——越南海阳 2×600MW 燃煤电站项目，参股建成了越南宁顺正胜 50 兆瓦风电和平顺 68MW 风电 A 段项目，控股投资菲律宾共享通信铁塔项目，参股东盟基金二期项目，与行业企业携手开发东盟市场。

中国能建积极参与东盟基础设施互联互通规划、投资与建设，为深化中国—东盟经贸合作、推动东盟地区经济社会发展贡献了能建之智、发挥了能建之力、展现了能建之为。

4. 中国交通建设集团有限公司

中国交通建设集团有限公司（中交集团）是全球领先的特大型基础设施综合服务商，主要从事交通基础设施的投资建设运营、装备制造、城市综合开发等，为客户提供投资融资、咨询规划、设计建造、管理运营一揽子解决方案和综合一体化服务。[①]

2023 年 7 月，中交集团与东博会首次牵手，荣膺第 20 届东博会首席战略合作伙伴。中交集团党委书记、董事长王彤宙在第 20 届中国—东盟博览会开幕式致辞中表示，中交集团秉持"让世界更畅通、让城市更宜居、让生活更美好"的发展愿景，愿充分发挥基础设施全产业链和综合一体化服务优势，全面深化与东盟各方合作。[②]

中交集团作为首批"走出去"的中央企业，也是参与共建"一带一路"的领军企业，在东盟地区交出了一份亮眼的成绩单，为中国—

---

① 中国交通建设集团有限公司官网［2024-08-10］. https://www.ccccltd.cn/aboutus/gsgk.

② 中国交建. 李强出席第二十届中国—东盟博览会开幕式并致辞，中交集团主要领导参加开幕式［EB/OL］.（2023-09-19）［2024-08-10］. https://www.ccccltd.cn/news/gsyw/202309/t20230919_210489.html.

东盟双边经贸往来作出了巨大贡献。截至 2023 年 9 月，中交集团在东盟地区累计合同额超过 530 亿美元，在建项目合同额 297 亿美元，设立机构 45 个，业务涉及港口航道、道路桥梁、机场、铁路、装备重工及城市综合体开发等领域，建设了马来西亚东海岸铁路及槟城二桥、柬埔寨金港高速、印尼泗水—马都拉大桥、马中关丹国际物流园、新加坡裕廊船厂、老挝水电站、斯里兰卡科伦坡港口城等代表性项目，打造了"中国港、中国路、中国桥、中国城、中国装备"等国家名片。① 此外，中交集团进入澜湄市场已有 30 余年历史，特别是 2016 年 3 月澜湄合作机制提出以来，中交集团全面参与澜湄流域经济发展带建设，在当地实施了超 130 亿美元的优质基础设施工程，仅在柬埔寨投资公路金额就超过了 32 亿美元，用中国方案和中国技术为澜湄地区民众带来更美好的生活体验。②

目前，中交集团正在参与建设新中国首条通江达海大运河、西部陆海新通道骨干工程平陆运河，并以此为牵引助推广西与东盟各国形成更紧密的合作关系，为中国与东盟合作升级、产业共建提供新动能。作为中国东盟经贸往来的深度参与者，中交集团愿持续深化与广西的合作，资源共享、优势互补，坚定支持东博会各项活动，推动中国与东盟合作迈上新台阶、结出更多硕果。

5. 广西柳工集团有限公司

广西柳工集团有限公司是国有资产授权经营方式组建的大型装备

---

① 广西日报—广西云客户端. 中交集团作为首席战略合作伙伴亮相第 20 届中国—东盟博览会［EB/OL］.（2023-09-18）［2024-08-10］. https://v.gxnews.com.cn/a/21288897.

② 人民网—国际频道. 中交集团积极助力澜湄地区合作［EB/OL］.（2023-07-04）［2024-08-10］. http://world.people.com.cn/n1/2023/0704/c1002-40027488.html.

制造业国有企业。主要从事工程机械及关键零部件的研发、制造、销售和服务工作。2021年习近平总书记到柳工视察，肯定了"柳工是标志性的装备制造企业，一家成功的国有企业"。冷链物流、食品加工业务为第二主培业务。柳工集团发布新品牌"桂味联"，持续研发预制菜产品，规划柳州智慧食品冷链产业园和上海智慧食品冷链技术基地等基地布局。

东盟是柳工最早进入的海外市场之一。经过近20年的耕耘和探索，柳工在东盟区域核心市场已建立起"专业化+本地化"团队，依托行业内最完善的本地化营销服务网络，现拥有亚太子公司、印尼子公司，在印尼、菲律宾、缅甸、泰国、越南等国打造了5个呼叫中心，并与21家经销商保持着友好合作。① 柳工设备在中老铁路②、雅万高铁③、中泰铁路④、马东铁路⑤、马来西亚联合钢铁厂等重大项目和工程建设中大显身手。柳工装载机在越南、泰国、缅甸等国家的市场占有率，连续多年排名靠前。

为提升其海外业务能力，在2023年10月，柳工机械越南有限公

---

① 柳工集团. 绿色高效｜柳工最新产品"闪亮"东博会［EB/OL］.（2022-09-16）［2024-07-30］. https://www.liugong.com/news/20220916.

② 柳工集团. 柳工机械助力中老铁路建设［EB/OL］.（2017-01-02）［2024-07-30］. https://www.liugong.com/news/20170102.

③ 柳工集团. 柳工"经典神机"为印尼雅万铁路建设保驾护航［EB/OL］.（2019-10-12）［2024-07-30］. https://www.liugong.com/news/20191012-7.

④ 中国路面机械网. 助力中泰铁路建设，柳工为"一带一路"战略再谱新篇章［EB/OL］.（2015-12-21）［2024-07-30］. https://news.lmjx.net/2015/201512/2015122111292252.shtml.

⑤ 国务院国有资产监督管理委员会. 柳工深耕东盟市场助力高质量共建"一带一路"［EB/OL］.（2021-09-16）［2024-07-30］. http://www.sasac.gov.cn/n2588025/n2588129/c20757270/content.html.

司在越南河内正式开业。自此，广西柳工集团全系列设备和配件不仅可以在 48 小时内运抵越南，也可为当地客户提供全面解决方案。① 从产品"走出去"，到品牌、技术、服务"走进去"，这是柳工走向海外的又一突破。

除了海外实实在在的战略举措，在国内柳工也抓住一切展示自己的机会。多次参加博览会，产品广受好评。2023 年，在南宁国际会展中心举行的中国—东盟农业机械暨甘蔗机械化博览会上，柳工农机携自主研发生产的产品 S713、S935 甘蔗收获机与 LT1404 和 LTG2004 农业拖拉机惊艳亮相展会。② 柳工也非常重视企业的第二主培业务，2023 年，在南宁举行的第 20 届中国—东盟博览会上，广西柳工集团食品板块亮相，为其食品业务打开知名度。③

6. 新加坡 ST Engineering

新加坡科技宇航有限公司（ST Engineering）集团总部位于新加坡，在全球 24 个国家/地区的 46 个城市设有 100 多家子公司和关联公司。作为全球最大的商用机身 MRO 供应商，其客户群包括全球领先的航空公司、空运和军事运营商。除此之外，该企业还涉及防务系统、飞行模拟、无人机技术、船舶建造和通信系统。

不仅如此，ST Engineering 在轨道交通、智慧出行以及智能公共基

---

① 柳工集团. 柳工越南公司在河内市正式开业［EB/OL］.（2023-10-04）［2024-07-30］. https://www.liugong.com/news/20231004/.

② 广西壮族自治区人民政府国有资产监督管理委员会. 柳工农机闪耀中国—东盟农业机械博览会［EB/OL］.（2023-12-27）［2024-07-30］. http://gzw.gxzf.gov.cn/xwzx/gzdt/t17760395.shtml.

③ 中国日报网. 广西柳工集团食品板块亮相第 20 届中国—东盟博览会［EB/OL］.（2023-09-22）［2024-07-30］. https://gx.chinadaily.com.cn/a/202309/22/WS650d0a0fa310936092f230c0.html.

础设施领域也有布局，已为中国以及东盟大部分国家提供铁道交通技术支持。其在轨道交通行业的地铁无人驾驶电子系统、机电设备深度集成、综合监控系统、线网集中调度指挥、列车车载通信系统与地铁运作管理系统领域保持着领先地位，是"六合一"轨道交通电子系统（包括综合监控系统、自动售检票系统、屏蔽门系统、乘客信息系统、通信系统、运作管理系统）的系统提供商。在中国大陆（北京、上海、广州等城市）、中国台湾、中国香港、新加坡、马来西亚、菲律宾、泰国、越南等国家和地区的 40 多个城市承担着地铁与轻轨项目，参与建设了 80 多条地铁线路。

在 2023 年，ST Engineering 宣布与中国物流运营商顺丰航空成立机身合资企业，总部设在湖北。① 双方的合作给中国运输业输送了"新"智慧，进一步提升顺丰航空的竞争力。不仅如此，在 2024 年4 月 17 日，ST Engineering 的地球观测和地理空间分析业务 ST Engineering Geo. Insights Pte. 有限公司（ST Engineering Geo-Insights）和安永企业顾问私人有限公司（EY Corporate Advisors Pte. Ltd.）有限公司（EY）宣布签署空间技术和地理空间分析谅解备忘录（MOU），旨在应对紧迫的环境挑战。

7. 比亚迪股份有限公司

比亚迪是一家致力于"用技术创新，满足人们对美好生活的向往"的高新技术企业。凭借研发实力和创新的发展模式，获得了全面的发展，并在电池、电子、乘用车、商用车和轨道交通等多个领域发

---

① 航空产业网. ST Engineering 与顺丰航空在湖北成立飞机维修公司［EB/OL］.（2023-05-17）［2024-07-30］. https://www.chinaerospace.com/article/show/4051a24348ab48fed4a88ed94e723983.

挥着举足轻重的作用。①

在东盟国家积极推动汽车电动化的时代，新能源汽车消费需求持续上升，市场潜力巨大。东盟已成为中国汽车"走出去"的重要目的地。比亚迪也追随市场需求的脚步，把战略布局到东盟市场。

首先与比亚迪达成合作的东盟国家是泰国。中国驻泰王国特命全权大使韩志强表示："泰国是东南亚地区首个出台电动车发展政策的国家，并在不断优化相关措施，这展现了泰国坚定绿色发展的决心，也为中国车企在泰发展提供了信心和动力。"② 泰国的多项优惠政策，使得中国多家车企与其双向奔赴。其中，比亚迪于2022年正式进入泰国市场，目前在泰国新能源市场中份额占比已经高达41%，并连续18个月夺得泰国新能源销量冠军。③ 比亚迪等新能源车企的进入，不仅为泰国消费者带来了智能绿色的驾车体验，同时也有效带动了当地的税收、就业、出口，并通过人才培养开展公益、慈善回馈当地民众。

不仅如此，通过建厂并积极使用本地供应商进行零部件生产，比亚迪已享受"EV3.5"政策。比亚迪也因此获得了泰国投资促进委员会的支持，其中便包含电动汽车、动力电池生产等项目。在此基础上，泰国投资促进委员会与王传福还均提到了泰国能够作为中国企业的基地，向东盟乃至全球市场发展的可能性。从地理位置上看，泰国区位

---

① 比亚迪股份有限公司—主页［2024-07-30］. https://www.bydglobal.com/cn/index.html.

② 重庆日报网. 比亚迪大消息：首个海外乘用车工厂峻工第800万辆新能源车下线［EB/OL］.（2024-07-04）［2024-07-30］. https://cqrb.cn/kaifang/2024-07-04/1963828_pc.html.

③ 每日经济新闻. 比亚迪第800万辆新能源车泰国下线王传福：未来将引入更多纯电、插混车型［EB/OL］.（2024-07-08）［2024-07-30］. https://www.nbd.com.cn/articles/2024-07-05/3455100.html.

优势明显，泰国市场除了对东南亚区域有较强的辐射带动作用外，还可以带动澳大利亚、新西兰、英国和南非等全球市场。以泰国为据点，中国车企能够将服务延伸至整个东盟地区，乃至全球右舵市场。除泰国之外，比亚迪也深耕柬埔寨市场。2024 年 7 月 4 日，比亚迪泰国工厂已竣工投产，年产能约 15 万辆。比亚迪柬埔寨工厂生产的电动汽车不仅可以供给柬埔寨市场，还可以出口东南亚其他国家。①

8. 上汽通用五菱汽车股份有限公司

上汽通用五菱汽车股份有限公司（上汽通用五菱）是由上海汽车集团股份有限公司（50.1%）、通用汽车（中国）投资有限公司（44%）、广西汽车集团（5.9%）三方共同组建的国内第一家国企混合所有制改革中形成的中中外合资企业。②

印度尼西亚政府积极推动新能源汽车的发展，宣布将电池电动汽车的销售增值税从 11% 削减至 1%，以鼓励采用电动汽车。在共建"一带一路"高质量发展的背景下，上汽通用五菱选择印尼作为其新能源汽车全球化的第一阶段中心，旨在打通东南亚、中东市场，并逐步向全球其他地区市场拓展。③

上汽通用五菱在印尼的投资建厂取得了显著的成果，同时带动了国内汽车零部件制造企业和其他中国配套企业共同参与国际化经营。

① 观察者网. 每日经济新闻. 比亚迪泰国生产基地投产，辐射东盟［EB/OL］.（2024-07-04）［2024-07-30］. https://www.guancha.cn/qiche/2024_07_04_740354.shtml.

② 上汽通用五菱 SGMW 官网［2024-08-09］. https://www.sgmw.com.cn/aboutUs.

③ 腾讯网. 七五观察丨五菱谈印尼新能源市场：初期阶段、自身需求驱动、本土化投入［EB/OL］.（2023-08-07）［2024-08-09］. https://new.qq.com/rain/a/20230807A07QLC00.

2015 年，上汽通用五菱汽车联合中国国内 16 家上游零部件供应商组团进入印尼市场，投资 10 亿美元，仅用两年时间，就在一片荒芜的土地上建起年产能 12 万辆整车的生产基地。① 截至 2023 年 7 月，已有 150 家印尼本地经销商建成并投入使用，已有 17 家国内供应商落地印尼零部件园区，涵盖汽车钢材、空调等主要零部件。同时，带动当地 48 家汽车零部件制造企业共同参与国际化经营，促进印尼当地就业及经济发展，仅五菱工业园区创造的就业人数就超 3000 人。②

在销售情况上，2022 年印尼汽车市场总销量为 104.8 万辆，其中上汽通用五菱印尼公司销售超过 3 万辆，市场份额达到 2.9%，同比上升了 17%。截至 2023 年，上汽通用五菱扎根印尼 8 年，在印尼带动近万个就业岗位，累计销量超过 13 万辆。③ 2024 年 1 月至 4 月，上汽通用五菱在印度尼西亚新能源汽车市场份额达 62.5%，多年来位居印度尼西亚新能源汽车销量排行榜第一名，已成为印尼市场上最畅销的中国汽车品牌。④ 凭借稳定的表现及卓越的品质，五菱电动汽车深受印尼政府青睐，多款电动车型成为 2022 年巴厘岛 G20 峰会、2023 年东盟峰会、2024 年第十届世界水论坛等重大国际场合的官方指定会务用

---

① 光明网. 中企助力印尼电动汽车发展［EB/OL］.（2024-01-03）［2024-08-09］. https://baijiahao.baidu.com/s?id=1787030652425311628.

② 郑柳芩、罗琦、阳继乐. 勇闯海外拓新道——探访上汽通用五菱印尼汽车有限公司［N/OL］. 广西日报，2023-09-15［2024-08-09］. https://gxrb.gxrb.com.cn/?name=gxrb&date=2023-09-15&code=006&xuhao=1.

③ 中国新闻网.（经济观察）东盟市场为何青睐中国新能源汽车?［EB/OL］.（2023-12-22）［2024-08-09］. https://baijiahao.baidu.com/s?id=17859749562529 35632.

④ 柳州市投资促进局. 印度尼西亚与上汽通用五菱加深合作打造右舵汽车全球基地［EB/OL］.（2024-06-18）［2024-08-09］. http://tzcjj.liuzhou.gov.cn/xwzx/lzdt/t19700101_3476077.shtml.

车，成为中国新能源汽车在印尼的一张靓丽名片。①

9. 印尼 PT Astra International Tbk

PT Astra International Tbk（简称"Astra"）是印度尼西亚一家知名的多元化企业集团。Astra 现在核心业务包括汽车、金融服务、重型设备、采矿、建筑和能源、农业贸易、基础设施和物流、信息技术和房地产，已与多个不同行业的全球领先企业建立战略联盟。②

Astra 作为印尼领先的汽车制造商和分销商，未来有很大的机会与中国汽车制造商（如比亚迪、上汽、一汽、广汽等）建立长期合作关系，进口中国生产的汽车零部件或整车，以满足印尼及东盟其他国家的市场需求，这种合作可能包括技术转让、联合研发、市场共享等多个方面。同时，作为印尼基建的巨头，在将来 Astra 会与中国企业共同参与东盟国家的基础设施建设项目，如道路、桥梁、港口等，这将极大有利于中国—东盟经贸的发展。不仅如此，在未来，Astra 与中国及东盟国家的物流企业建立供应链合作关系，优化物流网络、提高运输效率、降低物流成本。这种合作可能包括共同建设物流园区、开通国际物流通道、提供定制化物流解决方案等。

10. 顺丰速运

顺丰是中国及亚洲最大、全球第四大综合物流服务提供商。供应链综合物流（嘉里、新夏辉）、快递物流（仓配、医药、冷链、国际）和其他业务（顺丰科技、丰泰产业园）。

目前，顺丰国际快递业务已覆盖 84 个国家和地区，跨境电商业务

---

① 人民网. 中国电动汽车为印尼智能绿色出行注入新活力［EB/OL］.（2024-05-28）［2024-08-09］. http://world.people.com.cn/n1/2024/0528/c1002-40245172.html.

② PT Astra International Tbk［EB/OL］.［2024-07-30］. https://www.astra.co.id.

已覆盖208个国家和地区。2010年成立了新加坡顺丰分部，之后，顺丰开始开拓其他东南亚市场。2016年底成立越南分公司以及胡志明分部，2017年4月，顺丰宣布泰国分公司以及曼谷分部成立。几年时间，顺丰的国际业务先后覆盖了马来西亚、越南、泰国、柬埔寨、印度尼西亚等国家。

顺丰速运持续深耕东盟，与多个东盟国家开通航线。2017年8月27日，顺丰航空"成都—河内"货运输航线顺利开飞，首条国内直飞河内的全货机运输航线也由此启航。① 2017年12月2日，顺丰航空有限公司"长沙—胡志明"国际货运包机航线顺利开通，来自越南的多品类生鲜水产将搭载顺丰航空的航班飞入国门。② 2024年7月1日，顺丰航空一架B757-200型全货机从深圳宝安国际机场起飞，前往越南胡志明市，标志着"深圳—胡志明"国际货运航线正式开通，又一条直飞越南、链接东盟的货运航线。深圳—胡志明航线每周计划运行5班，可为深圳往返胡志明提供近280吨的航空运力，出口货物以航空快件、电商货物、五金配件、电子产品配件为主，进口货物以龙虾、青蟹、榴莲等生鲜农产品为主。③

除航线外，顺丰供应链依托南宁国际铁路港的地理优势、"中越班列"强大的运输网络，结合东盟前置仓的资源，致力于为更多"走出国门"的客户提供更快捷、高效的供应链解决方案。

---

① 顺丰航空.顺丰航空开通首条国内直飞河内货运航线波音767执飞［EB/OL］.［2024-07-30］. https://www.sf-airlines.com/sfa/zh/article_1468.html

② 顺丰航空.顺丰航空开通"长沙—胡志明"货运包机航线［EB/OL］.［2024-07-30］. https://www.sf-airlines.com/sfa/zh/article_1578.html.

③ 顺丰航空.链接东盟 顺丰航空开通"深圳—胡志明"国际货运航线［EB/OL］.［2024-07-30］. https://www.sf-airlines.com/sfa/zh/article_3809.html.

　　其中，在供应链中需求最突出的就是生鲜食品的运输。以榴莲为例，为了帮助泰国榴莲更好地开拓中国市场，顺丰与本土经销商的合作，采取预售模式，做到从源头把控榴莲品质，在气温和降水量等自然条件达到标准后，才会进行榴莲采摘发运，以保障100%树熟，100%好品质。顺丰以物流解决方案为支撑，探索出一条可借鉴复制的榴莲鲜果跨境直邮新模式。①

11. 马士基

　　马士基是一家全球综合性的集装箱航运和物流公司，集团主营业务涵盖航运、航空、信息技术、油气开发、工业制造和零售六大类业务。航运业是马士基集团的核心业务，旗下拥有超过730艘集装箱船，船队总运力达到1884万TEU，每年将1200万个集装箱运送至全球每个角落，占据全球市场17%的份额。

　　为扩大中国和东盟的市场，马士基宣布将投资超5亿美元强化东南亚地区的综合供应链能力。2023年12月20日，一列满载延安苹果的冷箱专列从陕西延安北站出发，该专列将途经西安，从广西凭祥口岸出境前往越南河内，全程大约需要8~10天。这是马士基首次开通中国与东南亚国家之间的冷箱跨境铁路运输服务，也是延安苹果首次通过冷箱班列运往国外市场。

　　马士基相关负责人表示，此次冷箱跨境铁路运输是集团在亚洲地区推出的一项创新服务，旨在为客户提供更快捷、更安全、更可靠的物流解决方案。不仅如此，马士基还推出了从越南到中国的榴莲冷箱陆运快线。未来，会继续扩大冷箱陆运快线服务的覆盖范围和频率，

---

　　①　顺丰官网. 如何吃到一颗"树上成熟"的东南亚榴莲？[EB/OL]. [2024-07-30]. https://www.sf-express.com/chn/sc/news/338.

促进中国和东盟间水果及多种产品进出口。①

除了供应链物流，马士基在中国的布局上海自贸区临港新片区2025年将力争实现集装箱吞吐量2600万标箱以上，其中国际中转和集拼箱量达到550万标箱以上。全球集装箱航运企业马士基在上海自贸区临港新片区设立国际中转集拼中心，该中心于2024年1月19日正式揭牌。将优化国际中转集拼平台运作模式，吸引全球拼箱企业在洋山特殊综合保税区内设立拼箱中心，允许开展出口拼箱、国际中转拆拼箱等多业态同场作业。②

（三）明星产品

1. 榴莲

（1）主要贸易现状

根据中国海关总署数据，2019年中国进口鲜榴莲60.45万吨，进口额超过16亿美元。鲜榴莲的进口量首超车厘子，成为中国的"进口水果之王"，也是中国与东盟的明星贸易水果。到2023年，中国进口鲜榴莲约142.59万吨，进口金额达到67.16亿美元，进口量同比增长72.87%，进口额增长65.56%。③

① 中华人民共和国国家邮政局. 马士基开通冷箱跨境铁路运输服务［EB/OL］.（2023－12－22）［2024－07－30］. https://www.spb.gov.cn/gjyzj/c200007/202312/480c81c923974e82a3e1b400a4fea8b1.shtml.

② 澎湃新闻. 马士基在上海临港设立国际中转集拼中，同步启动出口流向沿海捎带业务［EB/OL］.（2024－01－30）［2024－07－30］. https://www.thepaper.cn/newsDetail_forward_26194368.

③ 中华人民共和国商务部. 2023年中国进口142万吨榴莲，泰占65%［EB/OL］.（2024－02－21）［2024－08－05］. http://khonkaen.mofcom.gov.cn/article/jmxw/202402/20240203473632.shtml.

　　榴莲的保质期大约只有十天。因此，运输方式和速度对于榴莲贸易至关重要。泰国的榴莲主要通过海陆空三种运输方式出口到中国。自从中老铁路开通以来，每年4月开始，每天都有专门的水果列车通过这条铁路进入中国，并保持全程冷链运输，最终抵达昆明、重庆、广州等城市。此外，自2024年5月份起，中国将磨憨边境口岸的开放时间延长了三个小时，这意味着榴莲等水果可以更快地运抵中国，确保更多的新鲜泰国水果能够及时供应给中国的消费者。①

　　越南从2022年8月起，成为了继泰国之后第二个获得中国官方市场准入的新鲜榴莲出口国。越南榴莲享有较长的收获季节，并且由于较短的运输距离和较低的生产成本，具有明显的竞争优势。越南榴莲的市场准入填补了泰国榴莲季节结束后的空缺期。②

　　从2023年起，菲律宾也被允许向中国出口新鲜榴莲，成为第三个获准对华出口新鲜榴莲的国家。同年4月菲律宾首次向中国发送榴莲以来，中国对菲律宾榴莲的需求持续增长。当前，菲律宾榴莲主要通过空运和海运进入中国市场，从上海、广东、浙江等地区通关，但由于距离和基础设施障碍，从菲律宾到中国的运输成本通常高于其他东南亚出口商。

　　另外，中国的猫山王榴莲主要来自马来西亚。马来西亚自2011年开始向中国出口冷冻榴莲制品，2019年5月起则开始出口冷冻的整颗榴莲。目前，马来西亚榴莲产量的大约10%以冷冻的形式出口到中国大陆、中国香港以及新加坡等地，其中中国占据了马来西亚冷冻榴莲

---

① 刘旭. 中国东盟榴莲生意旺季更旺［N/OL］. 国际商报，2024-06-12［2024-07-30］. https://epa.comnews.cn/pc/content/202406/12/content_16336.html.

② 刘旭. 榴莲赛道，东盟四国奋力"争鲜"［N/OL］. 国际商报，2024-01-09［2024-07-30］. https://epa.comnews.cn/pc/content/202401/09/content_13285.html.

出口总额的 79%。

（2）新亮点

第一，东盟国家正积极扩展对中国出口新鲜榴莲。中国的"榴莲热"现象持续升温，为东南亚国家的水果商带来了巨大的商机。随着《区域全面经济伙伴关系协定》（RCEP）的生效以及中老铁路的开通，促进相关企业对华榴莲出口量提升至少 10%。时值中国与马来西亚建交 50 周年，两国于 2024 年 6 月正式签署马来西亚鲜食榴莲输华协议，马来西亚鲜食榴莲首次获准进入中国。据马来西亚《南洋商报》报道，截至 2024 年 7 月中旬，马来西亚已有 160 多家榴莲业者申请鲜食榴莲出口中国的准证。[①]

第二，运输方式和路径的多样化正快速发展。2023 年底，一批来自菲律宾的新鲜食用榴莲通过货机从马尼拉抵达浙江义乌机场，并在经过义乌海关的监管后快速运往当地的水果批发市场和各大超市——这是义乌航空口岸首次进口新鲜食用榴莲。与此同时，东盟国家的榴莲运往中国时有多重物流解决方案可供选择，除了空运，还包括公路运输、铁路运输和海运，并且可以根据不同的需求定制多式联运服务。

2. 新能源汽车

据中国海关总署统计，2023 年中国对东盟出口新能源汽车 32 万辆、同比增长 98%，出口量占中国新能源汽车全部出口量的 18%，东盟已成为中国新能源汽车出口和投资合作的重要市场。中国的新能源汽车为东盟国家的民众提供绿色环保的出行方式。随着东盟国家积极

[①] 中国新闻网. 马来西亚鲜食榴莲输华在即 榴莲业者盼更多合作 [EB/OL].（2024 - 08 - 02）[2024 - 08 - 09]. https://www.chinanews.com.cn/sh/2024/08 - 02/10262468.shtml.

鼓励新能源汽车产业的发展，并持续推出一系列的配套政策，中国新能源汽车迎来了"出海"新契机。

（1）主要合作伙伴

泰国是东南亚地区重要的电动汽车市场之一，也是中国新能源汽车企业进入东盟市场的首选地。比亚迪、长城汽车、哪吒汽车等企业已经在泰国建立了生产和销售基地。例如，比亚迪在 2022 年 8 月宣布进入泰国乘用车市场，并随后与 WHA 伟华集团大众有限公司签订了土地购买和建厂协议，计划在泰国建立其首个海外乘用车工厂。长城汽车也在 2020 年投资约 6.5 亿美元对其位于泰国罗勇的工厂进行了改造，以作为泰国的生产中心。哪吒汽车宣布在泰国建立生态智慧工厂，并于 2024 年 3 月开始规模化生产，年产能约为 2 万台。此外，广汽埃安在泰国曼谷发布首款海外车型 AION Y Plus，正式打响出海战略的第一枪。

马来西亚同样是中国汽车企业重点关注的市场之一。吉利与宝腾汽车的合作是其中的一个亮点，双方签署了区域合作备忘录，共同开发东南亚新能源汽车市场。宝腾汽车作为马来西亚的"国宝级"汽车品牌，于 2023 年推出了其首款新能源车型 X90，标志着品牌向新能源领域的转型。吉利与宝腾的合作得到了马来西亚政府的高度评价和支持，以推动马来西亚汽车产业向新能源领域转型。同时，借助广西壮族自治区首府南宁面向东盟的门户优势，smart 在南宁成立精灵汽车销售有限公司，助益 smart 品牌在东南亚市场蓬勃发展，赋能全球化运营布局。

印度尼西亚作为东南亚最大的单一市场，也吸引了中国电动汽车企业的关注。例如，上汽通用五菱印尼有限公司在印尼西爪哇省勿加泗投资 10 亿美元建设了汽车工业园区，旨在打造面向印尼和东南亚市场的生产基地。①

（2）新亮点

中国新能源汽车出口东盟市场呈现出"立体式"发展趋势，同时东盟国家为中国汽车出口提供了有力的政策支持，推动了中国新能源汽车在东盟市场的快速发展。第一，泰国政府积极推行新能源汽车政策。泰国计划到2030年使零排放汽车产量至少占汽车总产量的30%，并推动泰国成为世界电动汽车及其零部件的生产基地或区域中心。为此，泰国政府采取了一系列措施，包括降低整车和零部件进口关税，为新能源汽车提供购车补贴，并通过泰国投资促进委员会为新能源汽车整车、零部件生产和组装以及充电桩建设提供公司所得税减免。

第二，马来西亚政府也对新能源汽车的发展给予了大力支持。马来西亚政府对新能源汽车发展的支持，包括消费税减免和整车及关键零部件免税。根据马来西亚驻广州总领事馆投资处的信息，马来西亚政府设定了2050年实现净零排放的目标，到2050年达到80%的电动汽车采用率，实现90%的本地电动汽车制造率，并为此制定了相关政策。此外，外资企业在马来西亚制造业和部分服务业可以享有100%的独资权。

3. 机电产品

（1）主要贸易伙伴

据中国海关总署统计，2023年中国出口机电产品13.92万亿元，同比增长2.9%，占出口总值的58.6%，其中东盟占中国机电产品出

---

① 环球网. 打造生产基地，面向超大市场，中国新能源车企加速融入东盟 [EB/OL].（2023 - 09 - 15）［2024 - 08 - 05］. https://oversea. huanqiu. com/article/4EXyFmJppDu.

口总额的 13.2%。从广西来看，2023 年广西对东盟出口机电产品 1320 亿元，机电产品成为广西对东盟出口最主要商品。[①] 当前，中国机电产品对东盟的主要出口市场集中在越南、印尼、泰国、新加坡和马来西亚这五个国家。

2023 年，我国机电产品对越南出口 723.1 亿美元，同比下降 4.4%。对越出口以中间品和零散件为主，集成电路、手机零部件、计算机零部件、锂离子蓄电池、液晶平板显示模组等为对越出口的主要商品，2023 年以上产品合计占我国对越机电产品出口总额的近 1/3。近年，越南受益于全球制造业产能调整，吸引了电子信息、家用电器、光伏等行业企业的投资，带动中越两国产业合作和贸易快速增长，其占我国机电出口市场的比重也从 2010 年的不足 1% 升至 2023 年的 3.7%[②]。越南作为一个发展中国家，机电产品主要用于基础设施建设，加上与中国相邻的地缘优势和优惠的贸易政策，使得越南成为中国机电产品的重要进口国。

（2）新亮点

第一，中国与东盟产业链的互联互通能力加强。2020 年 11 月 25 日，《区域全面经济伙伴关系协定》（RCEP）正式签署，加强了中国与东盟之间的产业链供应链紧密度。中国与东盟各国鼓励本国机电产品产业在研发、系统集成等高附加值环节进行转型升级，并加强与东盟

---

① 广西壮族自治区外事办公室. 2023 年广西与东盟双边贸易规模高达 3394.4 亿元创历史新高 ［EB/OL］.（2024-02-02）［2024-07-30］. http://wsb.gxzf.gov.cn/yhjw_48207/gxydm_48209/t17943125.shtml.

② 中国国际贸易促进委员会广西分会. 2023 年机电产品出口市场 TOP10 来了 ［EB/OL］.（2024-02-26）［2024-07-30］. https://www.ccpitgx.org/index.php? a = show&catid=15&id=13695.

国家的垂直分工合作。例如，中国在东盟国家设立了境外产业园区、中小企业合作园区等，与东盟国家在中低端产业链上合作，提升了产业附加值和产业链融合能力，有助于发挥东盟国家的产能成本优势与中国制造业产业链配套完备的优势。

第二，在中国—东盟自贸区基础上建立互利互惠的贸易协定。在当前世界经济环境下，保护主义与自由贸易并存。为了进一步促进中国与东盟之间的机电产品贸易合作和发展，双方不断消除贸易壁垒，营造和谐稳定的经贸环境。具体而言，中国政府从政策层面制定了与东盟相关的互惠互利政策，地方政府不断加强与东盟各国的合作，持续吸引外资企业，促进了机电产品行业的发展。

第三，信息共享平台的搭建。2023年3月22日至24日，为期三天的2023国际产业合作大会（新加坡）暨中国机电产品品牌展览会在新加坡举行，来自RCEP地区的国际组织、行业协会、金融机构和企业代表共近600余人参加，133家中国企业参展，5000多家专业采购商观展交流，取得了显著成效。例如，通用技术集团在展会期间与多国代理商签署订单，与越南代理商签署战略合作协议。2023年3月31日，中国机电商会与马来西亚中华总商会共同举办"中国—马来西亚企业合作交流会"，双方企业代表逐一介绍自身业务，畅谈合作与发展，双方就项目研究、活动支持、信息共享、机制建设等方面充分交流并达成多项共识。①

4. 电力工程项目

中国—东盟电力合作与发展论坛已成功举办了十多年，既是作为

---

① 中国商务新闻网. 机电产品出口迈向更广阔新市场［EB/OL］.（2023-08-06）［2024-07-30］. https://www.comnews.cn/content/2023-08/06/content_29766.html.

中国—东盟博览会平台的延伸，也是服务于中国—东盟之间能源电力互联互通及高质量合作的关键举措。根据中国电力企业联合会的统计数据，2023 年，中国主要电力企业对外直接投资总金额 44.23 亿美元，涉及项目共 34 个。其中在东盟国家投资额占对外直接投资总额的 19%，涉及项目数量占项目总数的 26.5%。[①] 在中国和东盟各国的共同努力下，电力已经发展成为中国—东盟合作的重点领域之一。

（1）主要合作伙伴

电力是柬埔寨经济的优先发展领域，受到柬埔寨政府的高度重视。近年来，柬埔寨电力供应虽有所改善，但进口仍占很大比重，电价普遍较高，电力短缺问题已成为当前制约其工农业发展的主要因素。柬埔寨河流众多，水电资源丰富，中国电力企业在柬埔寨投资多为 BOT 形式的水电站开发项目。例如，中国电建在柬埔寨投资建设了甘再水电站，电站总库容 6.813 亿立方米，电站总装机容量为 19.32 万千瓦，年平均发电量为 4.98 亿千瓦时。[②] 甘再水电站项目进入商业运营期之后，不仅为当地提供了清洁的电力，还为当地提供了城市供水及灌溉等辅助功能。未来，柬政府将进一步加大水电和火电资源的开发力度以及与中国电力企业的合作，柬埔寨电力领域蕴藏着巨大的发展潜力。

其次，老挝经济的持续发展，电量消费呈显著增长趋势，2005 年至 2023 年间，用电总量比原来的 10 亿千瓦时翻了不止十倍。综合考虑老挝的经济发展、电力规划和历史用电情况等因素，预计老挝的用电总量将继续保持高速增长。与此同时，老挝政府制定了 2021—2025

---

① 中国贸易报. 中国与东盟电力合作呈现出活跃态势 [EB/OL]. (2024-06-25) [2024-07-30]. https://beijing.investgo.cn/article/yjdt/202406/727604.html.

② 中国新闻网. 柬埔寨中资甘再水电站发出泄洪预警 [EB/OL]. (2018-07-11) [2024-07-30]. https://baijiahao.baidu.com/s?id=1605695646503191200.

年国家电力规划，计划新增电力装机 4227.9MW，其中水电项目装机容量 2427.9MW，占新增总量的 57.4%。因此，水电是老挝未来电力发展的重点方向，而中国企业在老挝建设的电站项目也主要为水电站的开发。

中国电建在老挝投资建设的第一个 BOT 水电站项目——南俄 5 水电站，总装机容量达 12 万千瓦，项目自首台机组正式投运以来，已累计向老挝提供了超百亿千瓦时的清洁能源，每年大量减少二氧化碳排放量，成为首都万象和北部地区的稳定优质电源。① 此外，作为中国电建首个全流域投资开发的梯级水电站，老挝南欧江流域梯级电站项目总装机容量 127.2 万千瓦，是"中老经济走廊"、"澜湄合作"、老挝打造"东南亚蓄电池"发展战略的重点工程之一。②

菲律宾在以前主要通过化石燃料发电，煤炭发电量占总发电量的 50% 以上。为了减少对化石燃料的依赖，菲律宾政府大力推动水力发电、太阳能等可再生能源的发展，以应对能源需求增长和环境保护的双重挑战。作为一个以群岛为主的国家，菲律宾的地理条件非常适合水力发电，整个国家由 7000 多个岛屿组成，拥有 400 多条河流，水力资源非常丰富。2023 年 11 月 23 日，中国能建葛洲坝广西工程局承建的菲律宾良安水电站发电机组顺利安装完成。该项目位于菲律宾南部棉兰老岛巴科洛德市良安河，安装 2 台单机容量 5.95 兆瓦的卧轴式混

---

① 澎湃新闻. 央企声音 | 中国电建李燕明：为全球提供绿色、低碳、可持续的电力解决方案 [EB/OL]. (2021-11-26) [2024-07-30]. https://m.thepaper.cn/baijiahao_15579778.

② 中国电力建设集团. 老挝南欧江七级水电站圆满完成 72 小时试运行 [EB/OL]. (2021-09-22) [2024-07-30]. https://www.powerchina.cn/art/2021/9/22/art_7449_1223551.html.

流水轮发电机组，总装机容量 11.9 兆瓦。[①] 此外，国家电网公司参与菲律宾国家输电网特许经营权项目对于加强中菲两国在电网领域的合作具有重要意义。

（2）新亮点

第一，双方政府间已就电力合作达成一系列共识，如正在执行的《澜沧江—湄公河合作五年行动计划（2023—2027)》提出，加强各国电力规划沟通，共同促进区域电网建设、改造和重建，推动电力互联互通和电力贸易，向建立区域统一电力市场发展。

第二，区域合作的接连提出为中国—东盟电力合作注入新动力。中国和东盟国家在地理位置上毗邻，且有良好的合作历史背景，并在能源、经贸等方面有一定的合作基础。随着中国与东盟自贸区 3.0 版的提出，中国—东盟的电力合作潜力得到进一步释放，电力项目合作得到进一步深化。这在扩大原有合作基础的同时，也为中国和东盟电力领域的合作搭建更大的国际平台，为进一步促进双方的电力合作提供了机会。

5. 轨道交通项目

据统计，2023 年，西部陆海新通道跨境铁海联运班列共开行 9580 列，同比增长 8.6%；国际铁路联运班列开行 6784 列，同比增长 12.3%。[②] 这些轨道交通项目不仅增强了中国与东盟国家间的经济联

---

① 中国能源建设股份有限公司. 中国能建广西工程局菲律宾良安水电站水轮发电机组安装完成［EB/OL］.（2023－12－08）［2024－07－30］. https://www.ceec.net.cn/art/2023/12/8/art_52770_2529731.html.

② 封面新闻. 重庆海关：2023 年西部陆海新通道跨境铁海联运开行 9580 班列［EB/OL］.（2024－04－18）［2024－07－30］. https://baijiahao.baidu.com/s? id = 1796679862894889967.

动和发展，还创造了大量的就业机会和发展机遇。近年来，中国企业在东盟国家的城市轨道交通建设中扮演了重要角色，在工程建造、列车控制系统、车站建设、系统集成以及运营管理等多个领域提供了支持。

（1）主要合作伙伴

在马来西亚，由中国交通建设集团有限公司（中交集团）总承包的吉隆坡地铁二号线于 2023 年 3 月全面开通。这条线路总长 57.7 公里，设有 36 个车站，已成为连接吉隆坡及其周边地区的南北主干线，并显著提升了当地居民的出行体验。

新加坡地铁 T250A 项目的第四期双线 21.4 公里路段于去年 4 月由中铁一局完成并移交给业主方。该项目实现了"百万工时零事故"的安全记录，并因此获得了新加坡政府颁发的安全优秀奖项。新加坡陆路交通管理局轨道署官员和地铁运营公司负责人称赞该项目是轨道工程的典范。

河内轻轨吉灵—河东线是目前中国在海外首条集规范标准、施工技术、装备材料、监理和运营管理全产业链的最大城市轻轨项目。此外，中铁六局在越南河内轻轨吉灵—河东线项目中承担了培训工作，自项目启动以来，共培训了近 7000 名当地员工，为越南培养了一批轻轨驾驶、运营和维修的专业人才。

泰国政府为了刺激经济增长，加大了对基础设施的投资力度，尤其是在轨道交通领域。中国铁建、中国中铁、中国交建等企业已经参与到泰国的高铁和城市轨道项目中，例如中泰高铁项目。这些合作项目不仅促进了双边贸易，也为泰国带来了先进的技术和设备；中国中车旗下企业也为泰国提供了大量的轨道交通设备和服务，包括为曼谷

BTS 提供的 48 辆地铁车辆等。

（2）新亮点

第一，轨道交通产业链供应链合作深化。中国的轨道交通产业链覆盖广泛，包括设计咨询、原材料供应、建筑施工、装备制造、运营维护等多个环节，并延伸至增值服务。中国正加速其先进装备制造行业的国际化进程，向东盟国家输出高端轨道交通装备研发技术，协助当地发展配套产业，创造就业机会，促进出口增长，带动相关产业发展，构建起一个庞大的产业链生态系统。中国与东盟国家共同努力，建立跨境的轨道交通产业链、价值链和供应链，推动东盟区域内的轨道交通网络实现互联互通。

第二，注重轨道交通人才的培养。专业人才对于推动双方轨道交通现代化至关重要。中方为东盟国家的院校提供师资培训，联合培养铁路工程技术、运营管理以及新兴产业技术等领域的本地化人才。中国高校中的轨道交通专业面向东盟的轨道交通产业需求，通过校企合作的方式，为中国和东盟地区的轨道交通应用型人才搭建了培养平台，联合培养了"本土化"的轨道交通应用技术人才，服务于国家的共建"一带一路"和"走出去"战略。

第三，发展轨道交通数字经济。数字经济时代的加速到来，中国与东盟国家正积极寻求数字化转型和发展，促进新一代信息技术与传统行业的融合。双方在数字经济、城市轨道交通、大数据中心等领域的合作进一步加强，通过数字经济为中国与东盟国家之间的轨道交通合作提供强大的支撑。当前，中国与东盟构建"轨道交通+数字经济"的发展模式，利用轨道交通资源和平台服务的能力，为合作伙伴提供赋能，共同探索轨道交通产业的数字化转型和智能化升级。

第四，与域外国家开展合作。在 RCEP 和共建"一带一路"框架下，中国与东盟正在寻求与其他国家的合作，引入欧美等第三方的企业或资本，降低东盟铁路互联互通建设的成本与风险，防范和避免"场外因素"影响中国与东盟各国在轨道交通领域的合作，确保轨道交通项目的顺利进行，达到多方共赢。

（四）中国—东盟经贸合作新业态

1. 中国—东盟共建"蓝色经济伙伴关系"

"蓝色经济伙伴关系"是中国积极响应《联合国 2030 年可持续发展议程》的重要举措，旨在推动海洋治理能力现代化。[①] 长期以来，中国与东盟在海洋经济领域的合作历史悠久，合作机制日益完善。

（1）海洋环境保护合作

海洋垃圾治理。据统计，东盟地区 GDP 的 19% 来自海洋产业。然而，大量垃圾入海使得海洋环境受到了严重污染，地区渔业和旅游业等相关产业也面临严重威胁，这无疑在拖东盟地区经济社会发展的后腿。[②] 根据《曼谷宣言》，东盟成员国将在海洋垃圾治理方面实施联合行动，采取从陆地到海洋的相关合作措施，并加强执行相关法律，保持经常性的政策对话和信息共享，研究创新解决方案等。东盟国家共同向海洋垃圾"宣战"，有利于东盟地区生物多样性和自然资源保护，对东盟共同体可持续发展蓝图的实现大有裨益。

---

① 中国海洋发展研究中心. 中国—东盟蓝色伙伴关系的建立及其主要成就 [EB/OL].（2023－10－06）[2024－08－05]. https://aoc.ouc.edu.cn/2023/1010/c9824a444424/pagem.htm.

② 东博社. 东盟十国联手，首次向海洋垃圾"宣战"！[EB/OL].（2019－06－24）[2024－07－30]. https://www.163.com/dy/article/EIF2H9F00512DAHC.html.

海洋公园建设。近年来，自然资源部第三海洋研究所（海洋三所）发挥自身优势，主动融入共建"一带一路"，在海洋生物多样性观测、典型海洋生态调查、技术援助、研讨培训等方面与东盟国家开展务实合作，取得了一系列重要成果，为实现亚太区域海洋可持续发展做出了新贡献。中国与印尼方多年的联合调查换来了丰硕的研究成果，海洋三所的科研人员共鉴定出 1407 种海洋生物，并发现 4 个水母新种。此外，海洋三所研究员也多次赴泰国和马来西亚参与联合调查，获得了大量野外样品和视频数据资料。①

（2）海洋科技研发合作

近年来，中国与东盟国家在海洋科技领域的合作取得了显著成果。为了进一步深化合作，中国与东盟国家共同设立了中国—东盟海水养殖技术"一带一路"联合实验室。该联合研究与推广中心与泰国、马来西亚、印度尼西亚、菲律宾、越南等东盟国家开展海水养殖国际合作，开展海水养殖鱼、虾、藻遗传育种、健康养殖、病害防控等技术联合研究；开展中国和东盟国家重要海洋生物资源的采集工作并联合建立海水养殖种质资源库；联合开展人才培训和学术交流培养、技术示范等工作；举办中国—东盟海水养殖产业发展论坛和学术研讨会。②

（3）海洋旅游经济一体化合作

2024 年是中国—东盟人文交流年，中国—东盟迎春嘉年华活动于 2 月 2 日在福建省福州市启动，由丝绸之路旅游城市联盟提出的《加强中国—东盟区域性旅游合作的共同倡议》在会上发布。丝绸之路旅

---

① 泰伯网. 自然资源部第三海洋研究所助力"一带一路"建设纪实 ［EB/OL］. （2018-11-06）［2024-08-05］. https：//www.taibo.cn/p/53657.

② 中国—东盟海水养殖技术"一带一路"联合实验室 ［EB/OL］. （2023-04-07）［2024-07-30］. https：//smxy.shou.edu.cn/2023/0407/c2090a315756/page.htm.

游城市联盟于 2023 年 9 月成立，由文化和旅游部中外文化交流中心联合国内外知名旅游城市共同发起，目前已有包括柬埔寨、马来西亚、菲律宾、泰国、缅甸等 28 个国家的 63 个知名旅游城市加入联盟。①海南丰富的旅游资源为东盟国家游客带来优质的旅游体验，东盟国家已经成为海南的重要旅游客源地。2023 年，马来西亚游客同比增长 2028%，新加坡游客同比增长 1883.9%，泰国游客同比增长 1800.8%，东南亚入境游客占海南全省入境游客的三分之一左右。②

2. 中国—东盟共建"数字伙伴"关系

根据国家数据局发布的《数字中国发展报告（2023 年）》，2023 年我国数字经济规模超过 55 万亿元，2023 年数字经济核心产业增加值占国内生产总值的比重达 10%左右。③ 2020 年被称为"中国—东盟数字经济合作年"，双方共同发布了《中国—东盟关于建立数字经济合作伙伴关系的倡议》。之后，双方进一步推进数字经济合作，并于 2022 年通过了《落实中国—东盟数字经济合作伙伴关系行动计划（2021—2025）》，持续加强在智慧城市、5G、人工智能、电子商务、大数据、区块链、远程医疗等领域的合作。④

---

① 新华网.《加强中国—东盟区域性旅游合作的共同倡议》在福建福州发布 [EB/OL].（2024－02－02）[2024－07－30]. http://www.xinhuanet.com/politics/20240202/3ee251044cf14028b9af9ea446d3dba9/c.html.

② 阳光海南网. 海南向东盟国家旅行商推介旅游精品线路 [EB/OL].（2024－01－18）[2024－07－30]. https://lwt.hainan.gov.cn/ywdt/zwdt/202401/t20240118_3571851.html.

③ 黄卫挺.【光明论坛】激荡数字经济发展澎湃动能 [N/OL]. 光明日报，2024－06－21 [2024－08－05]. https://epaper.gmw.cn/gmrb/html/2024－06/21/nw.D110000gmrb_20240621_2-11.htm.

④ 中国社会科学网. 面向中国—东盟　助推数字经济发展 [EB/OL].（2024－03－25）[2024－07－30]. https://cssn.cn/skgz/bwyc/202403/t20240325_5741019.shtml.

（1）数字基础设施合作

实现数字互联互通，数字基础设施是关键。目前，中国—东盟信息港已建成 3 条围绕东盟国家建设的国际通信海缆、12 条跨境国际陆路通信光缆以及中国—东盟工业互联网标识解析节点、南宁国家级互联网骨干直联节点等 4 条通信节点，广西乃至中国与东盟国家数字基础设施互联互通能力得到大幅提升。中国东信参与建设及运营的澜湄云计算创新中心，已在老挝、柬埔寨、缅甸三国建立了云计算创新中心，实质性提升了当地数字基础设施水平。①

此外，中国电信也积极推动中国—东盟数字互联互通，不断加快广西数字基础设施建设，助力构建面向东盟的国际数字大通道。值得一提的是，在边境城市凭祥，中国电信还设置对越南方向的国际通信信道出入口局，目前已经建设多套传输系统实现与越南七大运营商对接，系统总容量超过 30T，已配置通道容量近 6T，能力辐射东盟泰国、越南、柬埔寨等多国，高质量共建"数字丝绸之路"②。

（2）数字化生活服务合作

智慧医疗领域。2024 年是中国与马来西亚建交 50 周年。春雨医生于 2024 年 6 月 5 日在吉隆坡与马来西亚科马集团旗下医疗公司正式签订战略合作框架协议，这也是中国互联网医疗平台机构首次出海，与东盟国家进行相关合作。后续，春雨医生会将先进互联网医疗科技

---

① 南宁市外事办公室. 携手共建"数字丝绸之路"：中国—东盟信息港助力中国与东盟区域合作提速增效［EB/OL］.（2023－12－14）［2024－07－30］. https://wsb. nanning.gov.cn/xxgk/zwdt/wsyw/t5795403.html.

② 人民网—广西频道. 广西电信积极推动中国—东盟数字互联互通［EB/OL］.（2023－12－20）［2024－08－05］. http://gx. people. com. cn/n2/2023/1220/c390645－40685273.html.

带到马来西亚，并在此深耕拓展，延伸服务海外华侨华人。①

数字支付领域。中国支付企业一直致力于在东南亚推广最新支付技术。中国支付企业通过搭建开发者平台、云发卡平台、场景服务平台、电子钱包等，"一站式"助力东南亚合作伙伴快速提高数字支付服务能力。目前，新加坡、泰国、马来西亚、柬埔寨、越南已落地18个银联标准的电子钱包，覆盖餐饮、交通、购物等支付场景。中国支付企业还积极参与当地支付基础设施建设，为当地建立全国统一、国际兼容的支付系统提供技术标准参考。中国银联支持菲律宾、泰国建成了本地银行卡转接网络，银联芯片卡标准成为泰国、缅甸的行业推荐标准。此外，中国企业还参与了新加坡全国通用付款二维码SGQR系统工作组的工作。②

在线教育领域。《广西面向东盟的"数字丝绸之路"三年行动计划（2021—2023年)》中提到创新面向东盟的数字教育合作，共建中国—东盟教育开放合作试验区，推动与东盟国家的教育合作向线上拓展。③目前，中国已与东盟职业院校开展了至少70个学生联合培养项目和两个教师联合培养项目，创办了8个职业教育论坛，组成了19个职业教

---

① 中国科技网. 中国互联网医疗平台首次出海春雨医生与马来西亚方建立合作关系［EB/OL］.（2024-06-05)［2024-07-30］. http://m.stdaily.com/index/kejixinwen/202406/04a4c4b8a78842d0a3b0785345610bba.shtml.

② 人民网. 中国与东盟国家加强数字支付合作［EB/OL］.（2021-01-27)［2024-07-30］. http://ip.people.com.cn/n1/2021/0127/c136655-32013669.html?utm_source=ufqinews.

③ 广西壮族自治区大数据发展局. 中国—东盟信息港建设指挥部关于印发《广西面向东盟的"数字丝绸之路"三年行动计划（2021—2023年)》的通知［EB/OL］.（2022-01-10)［2024-07-30］. http://dsjfzj.gxzf.gov.cn/zfxxgkzl/fdzdgknr_zfxxgkzl/zcwj_zfxxgkzl/fdzdgknrqt/t13106114.shtml.

育联盟，并在东盟建立 6 个鲁班工坊、42 个国际产业学院。此外，双方还根据不同专业大类建立国际职业教育合作平台。中国—东盟职业教育与应用型人才培养交流会、中国—东盟职业教育联展暨论坛、中国—东盟花艺技能国际邀请赛、中国—东盟大学生电子商务创新创业邀请赛等形式多样的交流合作平台，为各国职业教育从业者提供了分享经验、切磋技能的机会，为双方职业教育发展注入动力。①

（3）数字金融科技合作

十年回望，以"五通"为核心内容的共建"一带一路"已成为全球规模最大、参与度最广、福祉最多的国际公共产品。"资金融通"作为"五通"之一，是共建"一带一路"的重要支撑。数字货币的使用与贸易协定相结合，有助于降本增效、减少贸易壁垒和推动国际贸易的创新。② 2023 年 9 月 18 日，第 15 届中国—东盟金融合作与发展领袖论坛在广西南宁成功举办。论坛围绕"中国—东盟金融合作"签订多项合作协议。在桂金融机构与来自泰国、马来西亚、老挝、缅甸、越南等 5 个国家的金融机构或企业签订 6 份合作协议。海外项目融资签约金额约 232 亿元，主要支持老挝电力基础设施项目和马来西亚钢铁企业。多家中资金融机构与来自东盟各国的金融机构建立业务合作关系，在跨境结算、融资、金融市场业务、反洗钱、产品创新、客户

---

① 人民网. 中国与东盟加强职业教育合作［EB/OL］.（2024-04-12）［2024-08-05］. https://baijiahao.baidu.com/s?id=1796081980940407930.

② 中国新闻网. 金融助推区域繁荣——共建"一带一路"：中国—东盟跨境金融合作论坛在京举行［EB/OL］.（2023-11-09）［2024-07-30］. https://www.chinanews.com.cn/cj/2023/11-09/10109247.shtml.

和市场信息共享等方面达成合作共识。①

（4）数据跨境流动

数据跨境流动是数字经济时代的关键特征之一，在该领域加强国际合作有利于建立互信，减少政策壁垒，促进数据跨境安全有序流动。在《东盟经济共同体蓝图 2025》提出的建设东盟经济共同体五大支柱中，有关数字领域建设的相关内容主要集中在促进互联互通和部门合作支柱，要求各成员国推进区域产业部门的整合和合作。在信息和通信技术领域，明确要求各成员国进一步缩小数字区域鸿沟，提高区域互联网的普及率，推广智能城市和大数据分析；在电子商务领域，提出加快电子商务的区域合作，在电子化东盟（e-ASEAN）的框架下，促进电子商务的跨境交易。

（5）数字产业合作：外向型数字产业

中国—东盟数字经济产业园由广西投资集团旗下数字广西集团与中国科学院信息工程研究所、华为公司、南宁市人民政府、中航建设集团等单位合作共建。产业园聚焦信创产业，引入大数据、云计算、信息安全等一批新一代信息技术企业落户，陆续入园企业超 50 多家。② 2023 年，中国（广西）自由贸易试验区南宁片区累计入驻数字经济企业超 5700 家，包括华为、浪潮、腾讯等行业领军企业。中国—东盟信息港股份有限公司积极推动面向东盟的数字基础设施建设，在

① 中国金融新闻网. 中国—东盟金融合作项目协议正式签订［EB/OL］.（2023-09-19）［2024-08-05］. https://www.financialnews.com.cn/qy/dfjr/202309/t20230919_279211.html.

② 广西壮族自治区园区发展和投资促进服务中心. 中国—东盟数字经济产业园：构建数字现代化产业体系打造广西数字经济新一极［EB/OL］.（2024-07-10）［2024-08-06］. http://tzcjj.gxzf.gov.cn/gzdt/t18668486.shtml.

老挝、柬埔寨和缅甸建设运营澜湄云计算创新中心，开发中国（广西）国际贸易单一窗口、中国—东盟跨境征信服务平台等一批数字化平台，与东盟国家开展近 20 个数字经济项目合作。[①]

3. 中国—东盟共建"绿色伙伴"关系

我国与东盟国家通过绿色政策对接、绿色低碳合作、搭建交流平台、开展能力建设等措施，不断深化共建绿色丝绸之路。双方共同实施多项环境合作行动计划和战略，稳步推进《中国—东盟环境合作战略及行动框架 2021—2025》。2021 年 6 月，共同发起"一带一路"绿色发展伙伴关系倡议，旨在沟通绿色发展政策、借鉴经验，实现绿色和可持续的经济复苏。同时，搭建多层次、多领域的绿色发展对话平台，与东盟国家环境部门、机构、企业及国际组织共同启动绿色发展国际联盟，并成功举办多届环境合作论坛和合作周，有效促进了政策对话、经验交流、能力建设和务实合作。[②]

（1）深化农业合作发展和粮食安全合作

农业科技培训与绿色农业技术示范。推动绿色农业发展是中国和东盟在农业领域开展务实合作的一项重要内容。2023 年发布的《中国—东盟关于深化农业合作的联合声明》提出，促进绿色循环低碳有韧性的农业发展。如今，一批批中国农技专家与东盟国家当地农民、农技工作者正携手努力，为推进农业绿色和数字化转型贡献力量。据报道，近年来，中国与东盟国家相关机构开展密切合作，在老挝、越南、柬埔寨、印尼、缅甸建设了 5 个境外农业试验站，共筛选试种蔬菜、水

---

① 中国新闻网. 2023 年广西自贸试验区南宁片区新增企业 1.3 万家 ［EB/OL］.（2024-01-17）［2024-08-05］. https://news.sohu.com/a/752539058_123753.

② 人民画报. 推动共建中国—东盟绿色丝绸之路 ［EB/OL］.（2023-08-31）［2024-07-30］. http://www.rmhb.com.cn/zt/ydyl/202308/t20230831_800340936.html.

稻等优新品种 750 多个，累计示范推广面积超过 400 万亩，为项目所在国培训农业技术人员 1000 多人次。①

完善农业合作机制。农业合作议题一直是中国与东盟国家双多边合作的高频词汇。2023 年 9 月 6 日，第 26 次中国—东盟领导人会议上，双方发布的关于深化农业合作的联合声明明确，将采取务实举措，完善农业合作机制，提升区域农业粮食体系韧性，促进绿色循环低碳有韧性的农业发展，推动智慧农业和数字乡村发展，深化农业产业链合作，推动利益相关方积极参与区域农业合作。同日发布的《中国—东盟农业绿色发展行动计划（2023—2027)》表示，将鼓励公共部门、私营部门、学术界、小农等利益相关方相互协作，通过加强政策对话、联合研究、能力建设、人才交流等合作，加强农业资源保护利用，强化产地环境保护治理，提高农业质量效益和竞争力，促进农业可持续发展。②

粮食安全储备。中国和东盟国家的人口之和约占全球总人口的四分之一，提升地区粮食安全保障水平，将 20 亿民众饭碗牢牢端在手上，对维护世界粮食稳定具有十分重要的意义。赵广美介绍，自中国—东盟对话关系建立 30 年来，农业和粮食安全始终是双方合作的重点领域，在过去 30 年里签署了 40 多份双边农业合作协议，建立了 8 个

---

① 人民日报海外版. 中国与东盟农业合作持续走深走实［EB/OL］.（2024-05-18)［2024-07-30］. http://www.scio.gov.cn/gxzl/ydyl_26587/jmwl_26592/jmwl_26593/202405/t20240521_849079.html.

② 光明网. 中国与东盟农业合作前景广阔［EB/OL］.（2024-05-10)［2024-07-30］. https://baijiahao.baidu.com/s?id=1798628890770670412.

双边农业合作机制，共同实施了 300 多个农业技术合作项目。① 2022年，《中国—东盟粮食安全合作联合声明》发布，更彰显了各方对推动农业发展的重视和维护区域粮食安全的决心。2023 年是中国—东盟农业发展和粮食安全合作年，中国和东盟将共同致力于地区粮食安全，共同促进农业的绿色和数字转型，共同扩大农产品贸易，为全球粮农治理贡献智慧。

可再生能源利用与开发合作。中国和东盟各国在农村可再生能源领域的开发与合作，尤其是像沼气、生物燃料、风能、水电等领域的合作，对于节约能源、保护生态环境、缓解农村贫困、解决能源不足问题具有积极作用。②

在绿色能源合作方面，我国与东盟国家联手积极推进风电、水电、光伏等新能源项目建设，收获了东南亚地区功率最大的太阳能电站越南油汀太阳能电站、柬埔寨最大的水电站桑河二级水电站、越南最大垃圾发电项目河内朔山垃圾发电站、印尼首个水上光伏发电项目奇拉塔项目、新加坡最大光伏发电项目腾格水库 60 兆瓦水上光伏项目等一大批合作成果，有力推动了东盟国家能源绿色高效发展，支撑了东盟绿色低碳转型。同时，我国全面停止新建境外煤电项目，稳慎推进在东盟国家的在建境外煤电项目，推动已建成的境外煤电项目绿色低碳发展。

（2）开展应对气候变化与空气质量改善协同合作

清洁能源项目。东盟能源中心公布的最新数据显示，2021 年，可

---

① 贵州日报天眼新闻. 2023 中国—东盟教育交流周丨赵广美：加强国际合作共同维护全球粮食安全 ［EB/OL］. （2023-08-27）［2024-07-30］. https://www.guizhou. gov.cn/ztzl/dmjyjlz/202308/t20230827_82074565.html.

② 中国农村网. 牛盾：中国—东盟的农业合作⑤ ［EB/OL］. （2024-04-08）［2024-07-30］. https://baijiahao.baidu.com/s?id=1795779023483263730.

再生能源在东盟国家总能源供给中占比为 14.4%，发电装机容量占总装机容量的 33.9%。2016 年至 2021 年，东盟太阳能发电装机容量增长了 53%。东盟到 2025 年有望实现区域可再生能源发电装机容量占比达 35%的目标。①

中国积极推动建立中国—东盟清洁能源合作中心，推进清洁能源技术共享，加强金融支持，深化区域合作，为推动地区能源转型和可持续发展作出贡献。2023 年 11 月初，中企承建的印尼芝拉塔漂浮光伏发电项目成功实现全容量并网发电，这是东南亚地区最大的漂浮光伏项目，预计可为约 5 万户家庭提供清洁电力。中国与越南签署了电力与可再生能源合作谅解备忘录。中泰两国在风力发电、光伏发电等可再生能源领域的合作也取得积极成果。

森林保护与恢复。澜湄合作，是澜湄 6 个经济体共商共建共享的新型区域合作机制。八年来，中柬、中老、中缅、中泰、中越先后宣布构建命运共同体，澜湄地区实现双多边命运共同体建设全覆盖，树立了构建人类命运共同体的成功典范。② 在林草领域，中国与澜湄区域各经济体广泛开展多双边合作，与柬埔寨、老挝、缅甸和越南签订了林业双边合作协议，共同推进林业人才培养、森林可持续经营、野生动植物保护、林产品贸易、边境森林火灾防控、竹藤资源开发利用等合作。同时，国家林业和草原局支持亚太森林组织面向区域各经济体开展多个林业试点示范项目和林业人才培养项目。

绿色低碳合作。自 2009 年首个《中国—东盟环境保护合作战略》

---

① 光明网. 中国与东盟国家深化清洁能源合作［EB/OL］.（2023-12-06）［2024-07-30］. https：//m.gmw.cn/2023-12/06/content_1303592042.htm.

② 中国绿色时报. 互联互通 搭建澜湄区域林业合作桥梁［EB/OL］.（2024-03-27）［2024-07-30］. https：//www.forestry.gov.cn/c/www/lcdt/553216.jhtml.

发布以来，双方迄今已出台 5 部合作战略和行动计划，在环境和气候领域建立了成熟的政策对话机制，在高层政策对话、生物多样性和生态保护、环保产业与技术、联合研究等方面开展了各种合作活动，为南南环境合作作出了区域贡献。2011 年以来，中国累计安排资金约 12 亿元人民币，与 36 个发展中国家签署 41 份气候变化合作文件，其中就包括东盟国家。① "赛色塔低碳示范区" 是中国老挝双方积极应对气候变化的合作项目，也是建设绿色 "一带一路" 的务实举措。该示范区于 2022 年 4 月正式揭牌，随着中方援助的新能源车辆、太阳能供电设施等投入使用，预计每年可使当地减少约 1243 吨碳排放，相当于植树超 10 万棵。绿色可持续发展的理念推动万象新城发展成为老挝乃至东盟国家中低碳环保城市的典范。

---

① 光明日报. 中国和东盟应对气候变化合作前景广阔［EB/OL］.（2022-11-01）［2024-07-30］. https://news.gmw.cn/2022-11/01/content_36128275.htm.

五、中国—东盟（第 21 届东博会主题国）经贸合作

中国与本届中国—东盟博览会主题国马来西亚于 1974 年 5 月 31 日建交，2013 年建立全面战略伙伴关系，2023 年就共建中马命运共同体达成重要共识。2024 年是两国建交 50 周年暨"中马友好年"，双方发布了《深化提升全面战略伙伴关系、共建中马命运共同体的联合声明》。伴随着中马两国关系的深化，双方的经贸合作不断升级发展。

（一）国际经济技术合作：东海岸铁路项目

中马两国企业之间的经济技术合作领域广泛。当前，中国企业业务遍及马全境，在建项目主要集中在铁路、桥梁、水电站、房地产等领域，在公路、地铁、轻轨、通信等领域亦有新进展。其中，以中国企业承建马来西亚东海岸铁路项目较为典型。

1. 项目规划

东海岸衔接铁道（East Coast Rail Link，ECRL，又名东海岸铁路，或简称东铁）是一个在建的、连接马六甲海峡的巴生港和东海岸经济特区的双线铁路，旨在改善马来西亚半岛东海岸各州（吉兰丹州、登嘉楼州和彭亨州）与西海岸各州（森美兰州、雪兰莪州和布城联邦直

辖区）之间的目前只有部分铁路连接的交通联系，全长约 665 千米。计划用于客运——设计时速 160 千米/小时，以及货运——设计时速 80 千米/小时。全程 20 个车站，其中客站 14 个，客货站 5 个，货站 1 个。成本估算约为 500 亿林吉特（约合 780 亿元人民币）。项目于 2017 年 8 月 9 日开工奠基，2018 年 7 月暂停，2019 年 7 月恢复，计划于 2027 年完工和运营。至 2024 年年中，已完成铺轨近 200 千米。铁路开通后，从线路北端到南段的旅程将不到 4 个小时，而公路则需要 7 个小时。预计 2030 年乘客量 539 万人次。除改善连通性外，ECRL 还旨在刺激沿线工业、商业和旅游业的发展以及民生的改善。

2. 国际合作

ECRL 是"'一带一路'旗舰项目，中马两国共建'一带一路'重点项目，中马两国之间最大的经贸合作项目，中国企业海外在建的最大基础设施项目"①。2016 年 11 月 1 日，作为 ECRL 工程设计、采购、施工和试运营（EPCC）总承包商的中国交通建设股份有限公司（简称"中国交建"，CCCC），与马方政府为该项目成立的业主公司即马来西亚铁路衔接公司（MRL）在北京签署融资架构谅解备忘录和工程、采购与建筑合约（EPC）。2019 年 4 月 12 日，马国政府宣布 MRL 公司跟中国交建签署附加协议，涵盖东铁工程的 EPCC 方面。经过磋商，ECRL 在 2021 年进一步修订为 665 千米、502 亿林吉特、完工时间为 2027 年底。项目工程贷款主要由中国进出口银行（EXIM）向 MRL 提供融资贷款，马国政府为担保人。在铁路工程中，中国交建称与马来西亚当地超过 500 家转包商、157 家供应商及 91 家顾问公司合作，且尽可能

① 中国交建马来西亚东海岸铁路项目总经理部. 中交马东铁项目 2020 版宣传片 [EB/OL]. [2024-07-20]. https://www.cccecrl.com/zh/首页/.

在本地采购原料及设备。东铁的所有权马方 MRL 公司，营运和维护则由 MRL 和 CCCC 以 50：50 同等股权成立的合资企业共同负责。①

3. 社会经济效应

2024 年 6 月 19 日，中国国务院总理李强同马来西亚总理安瓦尔共同出席东海岸铁路项目鹅唛车站动工仪式时指出，东海岸铁路是中马高质量共建"一带一路"的旗舰项目；不仅仅是一条交通干线，还将在促进发展、创造就业、改善民生等方面发挥重要作用。在双方共同努力下，将把项目打造为优质高效、安全可靠的精品工程，建设成为"一带一路"合作的示范路、样板路，一条真正惠及民众的致富路、幸福路。中方也愿同马方积极研究东海岸铁路同中老、中泰铁路相联通，更好推进国际陆海贸易新通道建设，为提升地区互联互通水平、深化东盟共同体建设发挥更大作用。

马方高度重视 ECRL 对于促进马经济社会发展的重大作用，期望借助"中国速度"和先进科技，为马来西亚和地区国家发展注入强劲动力。作为马来西亚东西海岸之间的交通大动脉，ECRL 将有效带动沿线地区的经济社会发展，为大众提供舒适而便捷的出行和货运方式，促进铁路沿线商业、物流、贸易和旅游业的发展，改善民生，促进区域发展以及提升当地产业的竞争力。ECRL 也极大促进着中马两国的政策沟通、设施联通、贸易畅通、资金融通和民心相通，更紧密地形成责任共同体，利益共同体和生命共同体。

ECRL 是一条技术领先，绿色环保的高标准铁路项目，主动避让

① East Coast Rail Link（ECRL）Project, Malaysia Rail Link ［EB/OL］.（2024-02-19）［2024-07-20］. https://www.railway-technology.com/projects/east-coast-rail-link-ecrl-project/.

深软路基和世界遗产保护区。规划修建 160 多公里的桥梁和隧道，极力减少对沿途森林植被和野生动物的影响。

直接经济效应方面，预计建设阶段拉动马来西亚经济增长 2.7%，商品进口增长 3.3%，固定投资增长 21.1% 点。项目把东海岸诸多城市及经济区串珠成链，与中西部发达城市地区和重要港口相连，成为东海岸地区经济社会发展的重要催化剂。

社会就业效应方面，项目秉承属地化发展理念，与沿线社区当地居民，共建美好生活。土建工程属地分包与采购比例不低于 40%，为当地承包商设备和材料供应商带来商机；员工属地化比例在 50% ~ 70% 之间，并为属地员工提供良好的工作环境。承建方联合马来西亚建筑发展局实施中马铁路人才培训计划，为马来西亚培养储备大批铁路专业技能人才；联合马来西亚野生动物保护区开展铁路沿线野生动植物保护计划。

ECRL 建成后，中国交建还将参与项目的运营维护，引入中国先进管理经验提升项目，同时与当地政府和企业携手推进工业园科技园物流园以及交通导向产业的投资开发，推动产业升级，形成铁路沿线经济走廊和产业园的生态体系，促进经济社会可持续发展，与马来西亚人民共同开创美好未来。

（二）产业园区合作：中马"两国双园"

中马"两国双园"即中国—马来西亚钦州产业园（CMQIP）和马来西亚—中国关丹产业园（MCKIP）的简称①。作为中马两国领导人

---

① 中马"两国双园"等资料来源于中国—马来西亚钦州产业园和马来西亚—中国关丹产业园官网。

直接倡议并亲自推动的政府间重大合作项目，以姊妹工业园形式开展的双边经贸合作项目，以及中国—东盟战略合作框架下的标志性项目，中马双园以服务"一带一路"建设为目标，是继中国—新加坡苏州工业园区与中新天津生态城之后，中国政府与外国政府合作建设的国际园区以及"两国双园"国际合作新模式。

1. 中国—马来西亚钦州产业园

2011年10月，中马两国签署共建中马钦州产业园区项目协议。2012年3月经中国国务院批准设立，同年4月正式在钦州港区开园建设。园区规划面积55平方千米，以打造中国—东盟合作的示范区——"中马智造城，共赢示范区"为目标，定位为"先进制造基地、信息智慧走廊、文化生态新城、合作交流窗口"。园区设居住区、港口新城中心区、科研服务区、工业区和启动工业区等5个功能区，分3期建设。重点发展装备制造、电子信息、食品加工、材料及新材料、生物技术和现代服务业。

2019年8月，中国国务院批准设立中国（广西）自由贸易试验区，将中马钦州产业园区纳入自贸试验区钦州港片区范畴。中马钦州产业园区与钦州综合保税区、钦州港经济技术开发区实现"三区统筹"，中马钦州产业园区发展步入快车道，持续打造中马"两国双园"升级版，促进高水平对外开放和高质量发展。

截至2023年底，中马钦州产业园区已开发区域面积30平方千米，累计签约项目249个，累计完成固定资产投资295亿元，完成工业总产值938亿元，外贸进出口总额352亿元，形成了生物医药、电子信息、新能源材料和东盟特色产品加工贸易的产业集聚，园区在全国

230 家国家级经开区中排名第 83 位。①

2. 马来西亚—中国关丹产业园

2012 年 6 月 15 日，中马双方签署《中华人民共和国政府和马来西亚政府关于马中关丹产业园合作的协定》。2013 年 2 月，中马两国设立马来西亚—中国关丹产业园，规划面积约 12 平方千米，包含 3 个功能区：产业区、物流区、配套区（居住区、综合服务中心），以及分两期建设。重点发展钢铁及有色金属、机械装备制造、清洁能源及可再生能源、加工贸易和物流、电气电子信息工业及科学技术研发等产业。

马中关丹产业园区是中国在马来西亚设立的第一个国家级产业园区，被列入共建"一带一路"规划重大项目和跨境国际产能合作示范基地。由中国和马来西亚双方牵头企业在马成立合资公司作为产业园开发主体——马中关丹产业园有限公司，马方占股 51%，中方占股 49%，负责产业园区基础设施和公共设施的投资、建设、运营和维护。

至 2024 年 4 月，马中关丹产业园已完成土地开发 10 平方千米，入园项目 13 个，累计实现工业总产值超 600 亿元人民币，带动关丹港每年新增吞吐量超过 1000 万吨。② 目前已入驻园区的企业和项目主要有：联合钢铁一、二期项目、新迪轮胎、建晖纸业、中国港湾等。正

---

① 广西壮族自治区产业园区改革发展办公室. 中马"两国双园"：携手共建十余载"并蒂花开"谱新篇［N/OL］，（2024-04-22）［2024-07-20］. http://bbwb.gxzf.gov.cn/zwdt123/ywdt_1/t18316668.shtml.

② 中国—马来西亚钦州产业园区管理委员会. "两国双园"模式推动中马产业合作走向纵深［EB/OL］.（2024-06-21）［2024-07-21］. http://zmqzcyyq.gxzf.gov.cn/xwzx/mtbd/t18587783.shtml.

形成以钢铁、轮胎、玻璃、铝型材等为主的产业集群。园区依托独特的港口优势，以及地处东盟国家的中心的区位优势，利用马来西亚丰富的资源、完善的配套设施、便利的交通网络和优越的自然环境，大力发展港口物流及临港产业，努力建设成为马来西亚对外开放的东部门户、高水平的现代制造业集群和物流基地，进而构筑马中经贸合作战略发展的新平台，打造亚太地区投资创业的新高地，建设中国—东盟区域经济合作的示范区。①

3. 双园合作效应

10余年来，中马"两国双园"项目以建设跨境国际产能合作示范区，带动两国产业集群式发展为目标，结合当地资源和产业发展情况，立足中国—东盟，面向亚太地区，打造特色产业，推动中马产业合作走向纵深。

双方创立"港口—产业—园区"合作发展模式，以保障"两国双园"跨境产能合作物流运输正常运行。中国钦州港和马来西亚关丹港缔结为"姊妹港"，开通钦州港至关丹港双向集装箱直航航线，加强了中马"两国双园"海上物流运输通道，共同建设服务于共建"一带一路"倡议和西部陆海新通道的重要节点。

为促进"两国双园"的发展，园区进行"证照分离"、跨辖区"一照多址"等多项制度改革。同时，在两园区之间设立投融资便利化和跨境资金流动便利化创新试点，人民币双向流动便利化境内范围扩大至中国（广西）自由贸易试验区三大片区境外项目，人民币贷款

---

① 中国商务部对外投资和经济合作司，商务部国际贸易经济合作研究院，中国驻马来西亚大使馆经济商务处. 对外投资合作国别（地区）指南：马来西亚（2023年版）[R/OL].（2024-04-01）[2024-07-25].

境外范围扩大到东盟全域，以降低企业综合融资成本和拓宽企业跨境投融资渠道。

除此之外，得益于中马"两国双园"合作，钦州和关丹两市之间的文化交流也日趋频繁。两市轮流举办"两市双日"活动，在中马钦州产业园区共建"两国双园"国际创新创业联合孵化基地。"马来西亚—中国（广西）投资论坛暨中马'两国双园'建设庆祝活动""中国—东盟博览会主题国招待会暨中马'两国双园'建设周年活动""中马'两国双园'升级发展论坛""马来西亚棕榈油产业发展高峰论坛""中国—马来西亚企业投资与贸易对接会""中国—东盟大宗商品交易创新发展论坛""中国—东盟大宗商品供应链展"等系列活动，使"两国双园"从国家间合作向城市间、省州间合作扩展，从经贸合作逐渐向文化、艺术、教育、科技等多领域延伸。

（三）新质生产力合作

中国和马来西亚在数字经济、人工智能、新材料和新能源等新质生产力在全球或东亚区域具有自己的特色与优势。根据2024年6月20日中马两国政府《关于深化提升全面战略伙伴关系、共建中马命运共同体的联合声明》，两国将把握数字经济、绿色发展、人工智能、能源等新质生产力发展契机，积极开展先进制造业、科技创新、中小企业创业发展以及金融服务等领域合作。马方为中国企业参与马来西亚5G网络建设提供开放公平机会。双方同意围绕半导体价值链开展更多交流合作，维护全球产供链稳定。

1. 中马新质生产力合作发展契机

数字经济方面，根据《全球数字经济发展指数报告（TIMG

2023)》，中国在数字市场和数字基础设施领域优势较大，分别排名全球第二位和第三位，与共建"一带一路"沿线国家开展数字经济合作，与数字经济发展领先国家在细分领域展开数字经济合作的潜力巨大。马来西亚近年数字经济增幅在10%以上。马国政府在2021年发布的十年数字经济蓝图，计划10年内达到数字经济转型目标，预计在2025年为马国创造50万个与数字相关就业机会；数字经济对马国国内生产总值的贡献预计将从目前的23%上升至25.5%。[1] 通过吸引科技巨头投资以及数据中心和云服务供应商入驻，将马来西亚打造成为区域数据中心枢纽。这些，为两国数字经济合作造就良好契机，从数字金融到数字贸易、物流甚至数字健康服务等，两国都有非常广阔的合作空间。[2] 华为、阿里巴巴等正积极参与中马之间的"数字丝绸之路"建设，推动双方数字经济合作。

绿色经济方面，根据欧盟中国商会等机构2024年发布的《绿动欧洲：中国新能源汽车企业在欧发展报告》，中国已成为全球绿色经济的重要力量。《中国发展报告2023》显示，中国可再生能源继续保持全球领先地位，是全球最大的可再生能源产品生产国和消费国；中国电动汽车销量目前约占全球电动汽车销量的60%，位居全球第一。以新能源、电动汽车为代表的绿色低碳产业，成为中国经济新增长点。中国为全球提供了平价的绿色低碳产品，降低了全球绿色低碳转型成本，为全球绿色低碳转型作出重要贡献。马来西亚近年推动《国家可再生

① 中国—马来西亚钦州产业园区管理委员会. 马来西亚预计到2025年底数字经济将贡献25.5%的GDP［EB/OL］.（2024-07-04）［2024-07-21］. http://zmqzcyyq. gxzf.gov.cn/zmhz/mlcyzx/t18642917.shtml.

② 刘俪菁. 马中携手发展数字经济［EB/OL］.（2024-04-19）［2024-07-21］. https://cn.linkedin.com/pulse/马中携手发展数字经济-search-iu-rlqmc.

能源政策和行动计划》《绿色科技大蓝图》以及《国家能源转型路线图》等，努力摆脱对化石燃料的过度依赖，提高可再生能源比例，力争成为地区能源转型和可再生能源的领先国家。两国在绿色能源、绿色制造、绿色交通、绿色价值链伙伴关系等多领域的合作，可共促绿色经济转型。

人工智能方面，微软与领英联合发布的《2024 年工作趋势指数报告》显示，中国 91%，马国 84% 的知识型员工（全球 75%），如今在工作中使用人工智能来维持生产力、节省时间和激发创新。[①] 字节跳动（ByteDance）公司已计划投资约 100 亿林吉特（21.3 亿美元）在马来西亚建立一个人工智能中心。

新材料方面，国际半导体产业协会（SEMI）调查显示，2024 年全球半导体设备市场规模达到 1090 亿美元，其中中国占 32%。根据美国半导体行业协会（SIA）的数据，2024 年中国大陆为全球半导体的最大需求市场，约占 30%，国内半导体制造产能尚存在较大缺口。马国占全球半导体贸易的 7%，在全球半导体出口排名居第六；占全球芯片组装、测试和封装活动的 13%。2023 年马国的制造业投资中，电子电机产业占 56%。纳米技术、新半导体材料、基于可持续性的新工艺等，在马国快速增长。[②]

新能源方面，中国近年来大力发展包括太阳能、风能在内的可再

---

① Microsoft and LinkedIn. 2024 Work Trend Index Annual Report：AI at Work Is Here. Now Comes the Hard Part［R/OL］.（2024-05-08）［2024-07-21］. https://www.microsoft.com/en-us/worklab/work-trend-index/ai-at-work-is-here-now-comes-the-hard-part.

② 电子电气居全球前列 马国是投资者首选地［N］. 南洋商报,（2024-05-30）［2024-07-21］. https://www.enanyang.my/财经新闻/电子电气居全球前列-马国是投资者首选地.

生能源，新能源汽车行业的迅速发展。2023年，全球可再生能源新增装机容量5.1亿千瓦，中国贡献超过一半。马来西亚目前的电力消费主要依赖化石燃料，近81%的电力来源于化石燃料，低碳能源的占比仅为19.5%，其中水力发电占了17%，太阳能发电仅占不到2%，在清洁能源利用方面还有很大提升空间。马来西亚拥有丰富的太阳能和风能资源，在政府推行可再生能源政策的同时，顺应全球低碳化、可持续发展的新能源应用技术也在不断创新。其中，中国凭借在光伏发电领域的领先地位，为马来西亚绿色转型不仅提供设备，也提供了技术。如中国瑞兴能源、广核能源国际控股有限公司所属埃德拉电力控股有限公司、中国能建江苏省电力设计院有限公司等在马方的光伏发电项目。同时，中资企业凭借先进技术，与马来西亚在储能电站、制氢储氢一体化、氢能源智轨电车等方面的合作取得积极成效。位于沙捞越州首府古晋城市交通系统项目将采用由中车株洲电力机车研究所有限公司自主研发制造的氢能源智轨电车，中车将供应氢能源智轨车辆、信号系统、车辆段设备等。

新能源电池方面，国际能源署（IEA）2024年5月的专题报告显示，中国目前在全球电池生产和出口方面发挥着主导作用，2023年产量几乎占全球产量的80%，出口约占全球总额的70%，阴极、阳性活性材料产能则分别占全球产能的近90%和超过97%。根据研究机构EVTank的数据，全球动力电池出货量排名前十企业中，中国企业占据六席。作为实现2050年零碳排放目标的重要措施之一，马来西亚政府大力鼓励新能源，增加电动汽车充电基础设施，计划到2025年在国内建成1万个的公共充电设施，到2040年将可再生能源发电占比提高到41%。目前，中国的蔚蓝锂芯、星源材质、比亚迪、吉利汽车、长城汽车、哪吒汽车、珠海冠宇、亿纬锂能等新能源产业链企业已在马来西亚投资建厂。

2. 先进制造业合作

马来西亚在融入第四次工业革命（4IR）方面取得了长足进步。2018年启动的国家工业4.0政策（Industry4WRD），致力于政府、产业界和学术界的合作，旨在支持制造业和与制造业相关的服务行业成功过渡到工业4.0，提升生产力和产品附加值，创造更多的就业机会，并在制造业领域创建高技能人才库。此外，马来西亚数字经济蓝图（MyDIGITAL）、数字投资办公室、国家数字网络以及灯塔计划等举措，通过部署技术、改造劳动力和扩大端到端的供应链，加速制造业数字化转型，并为马来西亚在新进制造业方面吸引外资和技术。马方欢迎在人工智能（AI）、机器人、虚拟现实、大数据分析（BDA）、物联网（IoT）和软件工程等4IR技术领域做出贡献的投资者。[1] 先进半导体、电子电气、光电科技、纳米技术、医药、医疗设备等，是目前马来西亚政府鼓励外资进入的高科技领域及出口导向型制造类行业。

马来西亚早在20世纪70年代就吸引了许多外国芯片制造商，一度有"东方硅谷"的美誉，并形成了自己的半导体制造业生态系统。近年，马国引进的外商直接投资（FDI）大部分来自科技和芯片公司。目前，马来西亚占据全球半导体封装、组装和测试市场13%的份额，并计划于2030年将这一比例提升至15%。全球数十家半导体"大厂"先后在马来西亚布局。2024年4月22日马国政府发布《吉隆坡20

---

① 马来西亚投资发展局（MIDA）．制造业［EB/OL］．［2024-07-28］．https://www.mida.gov.my/zh-hans/industries/manufacturing/.

（KL20）行动文件》，计划打造东南亚最大的集成电路（IC）设计园区与数字产业中心，最晚在 2030 年挤进"全球创业生态系排名"前20 的国家。2024 年 5 月 28 日发布的《国家半导体战略》(NSS)，旨在巩固马来西亚作为国际领先的半导体制造和创新中心的地位，同时致力于建立强大的芯片设计基础。

基于中马双方的合作基础与潜力，以及贸易制裁和供应链挑战，近年众多中国芯片设计公司选择马来西亚作为境外供应来源，或海外封装枢纽，构建和稳定"中国—东盟—全球"相依的半导体产业链、供应链和价值链，以避免美国扩大对中国半导体产业制裁的风险。如马来西亚制造商 Unisem 公司，在马来西亚怡保、中国成都、印度尼西亚巴淡设有三个封装基地，且最大股东为中国半导体封装领军企业华天科技。又如，前华为子公司超聚变（Xfusion）近期与马来西亚的 NationGate 公司合作制造 GPU 服务器，以满足数据中心在人工智能及高性能计算领域的需求。

除了新一代信息技术产业，新能源汽车也是马来西亚以及整个东盟地区都在积极推进的产业。中国新能源汽车及相关产业目前在全球具有明显优势，2023 年中国占全球新能源汽车销量的 65%。中马双方合作是大势所趋。其中，吉利控股集团与马来西亚 DRB-HICOM 集团合作共建亚丹绒马林汽车高科技谷 AHTV，面向东盟等市场打造新能源汽车创新中心、新能源和新技术研发制造高地，推动了马来西亚汽车工业的发展。到 2035 年，AHTV 产业园计划实现年产 50 万辆整车，其中一半用于出口，同时，建立 100 万套零部件供应链体系，以服务全球市场的需求。比亚迪、长城、哪吒等中国新能源汽车主力军也在加快与马来西亚方面的投资合作。

3. 科技创新合作

马来西亚在电子信息、生物科技、太阳能、航空科技、石油化工和创新创业等领域具有较强的科研实力和竞争力。1992年两国签署《科技合作协定》，成立科技联委会。近年来，中马两国在诸多领域开展科技创新合作并取得积极成效，推动空间科技、中医药、人工智能、大数据、热带农业等领域科技成果转化与务实合作。马来西亚在与中国科技合作的过程中，从与中方开展的人工智能、电子商务、移动支付、生物科技、粮食安全、卫星制造、遥感技术等领域开展的合作中受益。近年来的中国—东盟技术转移与创新合作大会、中马政府间科技创新合作联委会、中马科技创新论坛、企业之间以及科研院校之间的研发合作等，推动双方在中国—东盟、共建"一带一路"等框架下，加强数字技术、绿色技术、生物技术、航空技术等领域进合作，拓展科技政策、联合研发、技术转移、科技人文交流合作，加强研究机构、科学家和研究人员之间的交流，共同组织国际科学家和研究人员参与学术项目和会议等，并以创新驱动产业发展，为双方经贸合作注入新动能。

4. 中小企业创业发展合作

中小企业是推动新质生产力创新发展的主力军。根据马来西亚统计局（DoSM）和中小企业机构（SME CORP）的统计，目前马国共有约120万家中小微企业（MSME），约占全国商业机构总数的97.2%，其中85%分布在服务业，6%分布在制造业。中小微企业多属于家族企业及华裔族群。2023年，中小微企业对马来西亚经济的贡献率为39%，对就业的贡献为49%，占全国出口的12%，但面临新挑战。根据《2030年国家创业政策》，马来西亚力争到2030年成为领先创业国家，中小企业对国内生产总值（GDP）的贡献达到 50%；提高中小微企业创新发展能力被列为五大目标之一，国家推动技术应用和数字人才培养，到 2025 年马来西亚 90% 的中小微企业将实现业务运营数字化。马国政府 2023 年通过 21 项战略和 184 项支持计划，提升中小微企业创新创业能力。马来西亚企业及合作社发展部（KUSKOP）和 SME CORP 以及众多的工商协会，通过中小企业政策、合作社发展、融资、培训、评级、资讯以及创业支持等服务，促进中小企业发展。2024 年 6 月，SME CORP 组织的以 "赋能中小企业可持续发展" 为主题的研讨会，超过 300 名来自马来西亚中小企业、东盟国家、中国大陆和中国香港的人士参加。中马中小企业目前在经贸往来、投资合作、商务项目、信息交流、政策倡议、会员互惠等多方面开展全方位合作。两国政府和企业可以通过两国中小企业服务机构，惠及量大面广的中小微企业，共促中小企业走向环境、社会和治理（ESG）实践的国际合作以及数字化发展。

5. 金融服务合作

资金融通是高质量产业合作的关键支撑。中马双方正稳步加强本币结算等金融领域的务实合作，以推动共建资金融通，实现高质量发展。2023 年 8 月，中国建设银行马来西亚分行与网联清算、马来西亚支付网（PayNet）在北京签署合作协议，以推动中马二维码互扫互认项目和人民币国际化，促进两国支付基础设施互联互通，提升经贸合作与人文交流。2023 年 11 月，中马跨境金融服务宣介会在吉隆坡成功举办。会议聚焦跨境人民币贸易结算、投融资以及人民币清算等多个领域的合作探讨和交流，推动相关各方在深化金融合作、推动人民币国际化方面迈出坚实步伐。同时，大华银行（UOB）等构建的商业数字平台，为区内企业国际合作提供现金管理、线上交易与实时追踪，以及一系列金融供应链在线管理方案，从在线融资申请到出货前后贷款以及跨境支付等环节。中马双方的金融合作推动金融科技和科技公司的发展，并促进企业的数字化转型。

附录　2023 年中国—东盟经贸合作大事记

（一）中国—东盟经贸合作大事记

2023 年 1 月

1 月 2 日，《区域全面经济伙伴关系协定》（RCEP）对印度尼西亚正式生效。至此，中国已与其他 14 个 RCEP 成员中的 13 个相互实施协定。

2023 年 2 月

2 月 7 日，中国—东盟自贸区 3.0 版谈判启动首轮磋商。

2 月 13 日—22 日，第 20 届中国—东盟博览会推介活动在印尼、泰国、越南举行。

2 月 17 日，海南自由贸易港推介会在印尼首都雅加达举行。

2023 年 3 月

3 月 9 日—10 日，中国银河证券中国—东盟商业领袖峰会在新加坡举行。

3 月 14 日—21 日，第 20 届中国—东盟博览会推介活动分别在柬埔寨、马来西亚、新加坡举行。

3 月 17 日—19 日，2023 年广西·东盟国际纺织服装产业博览会在广西南宁举行。

3 月 22 日，2023 国际产业合作大会（新加坡）暨中国机电产品品牌展览会在新加坡开幕。

3 月 29 日—4 月 8 日，第 20 届中国—东盟博览会推介活动分别在文莱、老挝、马来西亚、缅甸、菲律宾、新加坡、越南举行。

2023 年 4 月

4 月 4 日—5 日，第 20 届中国—东盟博览会新加坡巡展暨国际陆海贸易新通道、"桂品出海"活动在新加坡举行。

4 月 10 日—12 日，中国—东盟自贸区 3.0 版第二轮谈判在泰国曼谷举行。

4 月 20 日—22 日，第 20 届中国—东盟博览会推介活动在柬埔寨举行。

4 月 24 日—26 日，第 20 届中国—东盟博览会老挝巡展暨"桂品出海"活动在老挝万象举行。

4 月 26 日，中国—东盟数字农业论坛在山东省潍坊市举行。

2023 年 5 月

5 月 10 日—11 日，第 42 届东盟峰会在印尼东努沙登加拉省举行。

5 月 17 日，中国·东盟国家落实《南海各方行为宣言》第 20 次高官会在越南下龙举行。

5 月 19 日，第 12 届中国—东盟矿业合作论坛暨推介展示会在广西南宁市开幕。

5 月 24 日—26 日，第 29 次中国—东盟高官磋商在中国深圳举行。

2023 年 6 月

6 月 2 日，《区域全面经济伙伴关系协定》（RCEP）对菲律宾正式生效，至此 RCEP 对 15 个签署国全面生效，协定进入全面实施新阶段。

6月7日—9日，侨连五洲·七彩云南——第19届东盟华商会在云南举办。

6月10日—17日，第20届中国—东盟博览会推介活动在沙特阿拉伯、阿联酋举行。

6月12日，2023年东盟与中日韩区域经济展望（AREO）中国论坛在北京举办。

6月24日—26日，第16届世界华商大会在泰国曼谷成功举行。

6月25日，中国—东盟自贸区3.0版第三轮谈判开幕式在云南昆明举行。

6月26日，第17届中国—东盟社会发展与减贫论坛在广西北海开幕。

2023年7月

7月3日，第5届澜沧江—湄公河商务论坛在广西南宁举行。

7月4日，第20届中国—东盟博览会、中国—东盟商务与投资峰会推介招待会在北京中国—东盟中心举办。

7月4日—5日，中国—东盟新兴产业论坛在深圳举办。

7月12日—14日，中国—东盟博览会马来西亚巡展暨"桂品出海"活动在马来西亚吉隆坡举行。

2023年8月

8月10日，中国—东盟跨境供应链创新发展论坛在广西南宁举办。

8月16日，第7届中国—南亚博览会暨第27届中国昆明进出口商品交易会在缅甸举办。

2023 年 9 月

9 月 5 日—7 日，第 43 届东盟峰会在轮值主席国印尼首都雅加达开幕。其间举办第 26 次中国—东盟（10+1）、东盟与中日韩（10+3）领导人会议和第 18 届东亚峰会（EAS）等。

9 月 14 日，2023 中国—东盟产业合作区投资经贸合作洽谈会、第 4 届中国—东盟石油和化工国际合作大会暨产业链招商推介活动在广西钦州举行。

9 月 14 日，第 7 届中国—东盟药品合作发展高峰论坛在广西防城港开幕。

9 月 15 日，中国—东盟环境合作论坛、"一带一路"海关食品安全合作研讨会分别在广西南宁举行。

9 月 16 日—19 日，第 20 届中国—东盟博览会和中国—东盟商务与投资峰会在广西南宁举行。

9 月 16 日，首届中国—东盟建设部长圆桌会议、第 7 届中国—东盟农业合作论坛、第 14 届中国—东盟知识产权局局长会议、2023 中国—东盟丝路电商论坛、第 3 届中国—东盟气象合作论坛、第 3 届中国—东盟和平利用核技术论坛、2023 中国—东盟统计论坛分别在广西南宁举行。

9 月 17 日，中国—东盟博览会"制度型开放：区域经济发展新格局"主题边会、第 3 届 RCEP 经贸合作工商高峰论坛、中国—东盟产能与投资合作论坛、2023 中国—东盟产业合作暨"两国双园"项目分享圆桌会分别在广西南宁举行。

9 月 18 日，第 3 届中国—东盟民航合作论坛、第 15 届中国—东盟金融合作与发展领袖论坛在广西南宁举行。

2023 年 9 月 19 日，第 4 届中国（广西）—东盟人工智能大会在广西南宁召开。

2023 年 10 月

10 月 10 日，中国—东盟思想库网络 2023 年年会在印尼日惹举行。

10 月 12 日，2023 中国—东盟国际标准化论坛在广西柳州举行。

10 月 15 日，2023 中国—东盟传统医药健康旅游国际论坛在广西巴马举行。

10 月 17 日，习近平总书记在北京人民大会堂同来华出席第三届"一带一路"国际合作高峰论坛并进行国事访问的印度尼西亚总统佐科举行会谈。

10 月 18 日，习近平总书记出席第三届"一带一路"国际合作高峰论坛开幕式并发表题为《建设开放包容、互联互通、共同发展的世界》的主旨演讲。

10 月 18 日，中华人民共和国和印度尼西亚共和国发表关于深化全方位战略合作的联合声明。

10 月 18 日，2023 中国—东盟可持续发展合作圆桌会议在广西南宁举行并发布《中国—东盟发展报告 2023》。

10 月 25 日—10 月 29 日，中国—东盟自贸区 3.0 版第四轮谈判在印度尼西亚万隆举行。

10 月 25 日—29 日，第 21 届中国—东盟博览会推介活动在文莱举行。

2023 年 11 月

11 月 6 日，"一带一路"互联互通与携手构建中老命运共同体高端论坛在老挝万象举行。

11 月 8 日，2023 中国—东盟金融合作论坛在北京举办。

2023 年 12 月

12 月 7 日，澜沧江—湄公河合作第八次外长会在北京举行。

12 月 8 日—10 日，2023 中国—东盟大健康产业峰会暨大健康产业博览会在南宁举行。

12 月 12 日—14 日，第 21 届中国—东盟博览会推介活动在印尼举行。

12 月 12 日，"海南自由贸易港与东盟经贸合作"专题论坛在马来西亚吉隆坡召开。

12 月 14 日，中国—东盟蓝色经济合作研讨会在印度尼西亚雅加达举行。

12 月 25 日，澜沧江—湄公河合作第四次领导人会议通过视频举行，会议发表《澜湄合作第四次领导人会议内比都宣言》和《澜沧江—湄公河合作五年行动计划（2023—2027）》。

（二）　中国与东盟 10 国经贸合作大事记

文莱

2 月 2 日，广西—文莱经济走廊联合工作委员会第三次会议以线上视频形式召开。

7 月 8 日，文莱摩拉港至广西北部湾港集装箱航线正式首航。

7 月 26 日，中国政府恢复对文莱公民 15 天免签入境政策。

12 月 15 日，两国签署文莱输华野生、养殖水产品议定书，文莱新增 134 种输华水产品。

柬埔寨

2 月 10 日，国家主席习近平在钓鱼台国宾馆会见柬埔寨首相洪森，就构建新时代中柬命运共同体及共同关心的国际和地区问题深入交换意见。

2月11日，中华人民共和国和柬埔寨王国就关于构建新时代中柬命运共同体发表联合声明。

2月24日，国家主席习近平和夫人彭丽媛在钓鱼台国宾馆养源斋亲切会见柬埔寨国王西哈莫尼和太后莫尼列。

5月11日，柬埔寨胡椒已完成输华所有程序，获准输华。

8月1日，柬埔寨所有水产品和食用水生动物已完成输华准入。

9月15日，柬埔寨鲜食椰子已完成输华准入。

9月17日，柬埔寨首相洪玛奈在中国南宁出席第20届中国—东盟博览会。

10月16日，暹粒吴哥国际机场正式通航运营，首日接待来自中泰两国约17个航班。

11月1日，第三届中柬智库高端论坛在北京举办。

12月12日，中国银行金边分行获准担任柬埔寨人民币清算行。

12月19日，"丝路心相通"中柬民生合作系列活动启动仪式在柬埔寨首都金边举行。

印度尼西亚

2月21日，印度尼西亚—福州经贸对接会暨项目签约活动在雅加达举行。

9月7日，中印尼合作建设的雅加达至万隆高速铁路开通运行，中印尼共建"一带一路"取得重大标志性成果。

9月17日，印尼副总统马鲁夫在中国南宁出席第20届中国—东盟博览会。

10 月 2 日，印度尼西亚总统佐科在印尼首都雅加达哈利姆高铁站宣布中印尼合建的雅万高铁正式启用。

11 月 23 日，第 5 届中国（印尼）贸易博览会在雅加达国际会展中心开幕，同期举办中国—印尼新能源产业对接会、中国印尼新能源汽车行业合作交流论坛和中国（印尼）智慧交通及能源产业展览会。

老挝

3 月 22 日，中国援老挝远程教育工程（技术援助部分）项目在老挝首都万象启动。

3 月 29 日，中国（云南）老挝经贸合作项目签约仪式在老挝首都万象举办。

4 月 13 日，中老铁路"澜沧号"国际旅客列车首发仪式在老挝首都万象举行。

4 月 24 日—26 日，第 20 届中国—东盟博览会老挝巡展暨"桂品出海"活动在老挝首都万象隆重举行。

5 月 29 日，中国—老挝经济、贸易和技术合作委员会第 11 次会议在北京召开。

8 月 22 日，中老商务合作洽谈会在万象老挝国家工商会举办。

9 月 17 日，老挝总理宋赛在中国南宁出席第 20 届中国—东盟博览会。

11 月 14 日，第 7 届老挝政府与中资企业对话会在老挝首都万象举行。

12 月 8 日，中老铁路"云贵·澜湄线"国际货运专列首发。

12 月 11 日，中国援老挝农村扶贫设施建设项目二期开工仪式在老挝琅勃拉邦省举行。

马来西亚

6月1日，中国广西—马来西亚彭亨州农产品及旅游专场对接会在广西南宁举办。

9月17日，马来西亚总理安瓦尔在中国南宁出席第20届中国—东盟博览会。

11月1日，"构建中马命运共同体：机遇、前景与挑战"国际学术研讨会在马来西亚吉隆坡顺利举行。

11月27日，中国·海南自贸港—马来西亚双向合作推介会在马来西亚吉隆坡举行。

缅甸

2月15日，滇缅经贸合作推介会在缅甸仰光举办。

3月1日，云南机械设备进出口公司联合体同缅甸电力部合作的风电项目合作协议签字仪式在内比都举行。

6月29日，中国（温州）—缅甸经贸合作交流会在缅甸仰光举行。

10月26日，"中缅共建'一带一路'携手共享发展繁荣"研讨会在缅甸仰光举行。

菲律宾

1月3日—5日，应中华人民共和国主席习近平邀请，菲律宾共和国总统费迪南德·罗慕尔德兹·马科斯对中国进行国事访问，1月5日中菲两国发表联合声明。

1月30日，中交集团党委书记、董事长王彤宙在马尼拉拜会菲律宾总统费迪南德·罗慕尔德兹·马科斯，双方就大交通基础设施建设、大城市综合治理等领域合作座谈交流。

3月13日，中国福建—菲律宾经贸合作推介会在马尼拉钻石大酒店举行。

8月9日，菲律宾达沃市与山东省泰安市结为友好城市。

新加坡

3月15日，"海南自贸港金融产业专题推介会"在新加坡举办。

4月1日，商务部部长王文涛与新加坡贸工部长颜金勇共同签署了《中华人民共和国商务部和新加坡贸易与工业部关于宣布实质性完成中国—新加坡自由贸易协定升级后续谈判的谅解备忘录》，确认实质性完成两国自贸协定升级后续谈判。

10月19日，中国—新加坡首个全环节跨境贸易数字化实单试点落地。

11月6日，第6届新中经贸与投资论坛在上海举办。

12月4日，中新双边投资促进委员会第七次联席会议在北京召开。

泰国

4月3日—7日，泰国投资促进委员会（BOI）秘书长纳里率团赴中国进行路演。

7月9日，中国（汕头）泰国经贸文化合作交流会在曼谷举行。

8月16日，泰国尚泰零售集团（CRC）与蚂蚁金服合作，引入支付宝钱包服务。

9月17日，泰国副总理兼商业部长普坦在中国南宁出席第20届中国—东盟博览会。

9月19日，中国—泰国商务对接交流会在泰国驻华大使馆召开。

10月18日，由泰国外交部、泰国驻华大使馆主办的"泰—中商务合作圆桌论坛"在北京举行。

10 月 25 日,中国石化与泰国石油公司 SUSCO 在拉差达披色开设第一家泰中加油站 SINOPEC SUSCO。

11 月 29 日,中泰汽车产业合作发展交流会暨中国汽车技术研究中心有限公司东南亚代表处启动会在泰国曼谷成功举办。

12 月 10 日,阿里巴巴团队与泰国数字经济与社会部部长巴舍会面,洽谈合作以提升泰国云端技术水平。

12 月 10 日,首班"泰—中俄欧"货运列车正式开通运营。

12 月 18 日,由华为公司与泰国数字经济与社会部联合举办的2023 年泰国华为云 AI 峰会在泰国曼谷诗丽吉王后国家会议中心举行,双方签署数字化转型合作谅解备忘录。

越南

1 月 8 日,中方全面恢复南溪河铁路口岸、中越红河公路大桥等边境口岸活动。

4 月 18 日,越南领先信息技术服务提供商 FPT 软件公司在广西南宁开设近岸开发中心。

6 月 7 日,中国(广西)—越南经贸交流专场洽谈会在广西南宁举办。

6 月 27 日,2023 年广西·凭祥中越边关旅游节在广西崇左凭祥市开幕。

9 月 15 日,中越德天(板约)瀑布跨境旅游合作区试运营启动仪式在合作区两国查验点的边界线上举行,中越德天(板约)瀑布跨境旅游合作区启动试运营。

9 月 17 日,越南总理范明政在中国南宁出席第 20 届中国—东盟博览会。

11 月 27 日，商务部部长王文涛在越南河内与越工贸部部长阮鸿延共同主持召开中越经贸合委会第十二次会议。

11 月 30 日，第 15 届越中（芒街—东兴）国际商贸·旅游博览会在越南广宁省芒街市开幕。

12 月 13 日，中华人民共和国和越南社会主义共和国发表关于进一步深化和提升全面战略合作伙伴关系、构建具有战略意义的中越命运共同体的联合声明。

12 月 28 日，越南茶岭—中国龙邦（含越南那弄—中国那西通道）国际性口岸正式开通。

本书章节分工

写在前面的话（代序）　韦朝晖　李光辉

综述　黄革

第一章、第三章　韦倩青（货物贸易）、张伟豪（双向投资）、王娟（服务贸易）、刘主光（中国—东盟自贸区3.0版）

第二章　韦苏健、程成

第四章　陈伟宏

第五章　李红

附录（大事记）　蒋诗琪

Blue Book of CHINA–ASEAN EXPO

Vision on China–ASEAN Economic and Trade Cooperation 2024—2025

CAEXPO

CHINA–ASEAN EXPO SECRETARIAT

CHINA–ASEAN SCHOOL OF ECONOMICS OF

GUANGXI UNIVERSITY

CONTENTS

Preface

China and the ASEAN countries share a close geographical proximity and cultural affinity, nurturing a longstanding tradition of amicable interactions. The relationship between China and ASEAN have witnessed leapfrog development, with the initiation of dialogue relations in 1991, the establishment of strategic partnership in 2003, and the upgrade to comprehensive strategic partnership in 2021. It has become the most successful and dynamic example of regional cooperation in the Asia - Pacific region and a vivid example of promoting the building of building a community with a shared future for mankind.

The China-ASEAN Expo (CAEXPO), co-hosted by the economic and trade authorities of China and the 10 ASEAN countriesalong with the ASEAN Secretariat, and organized by Guangxi Zhuang Autonomous Region, has gone through 20 years of history. It has grown alongside the friendly relations between China and ASEAN, and in tandem with the China - ASEAN Free Trade Area. The Expo has become a significant open platform for China-ASEAN, an accelerator for the construction of the China-ASEAN Free Trade Area, the "Nanning Channel" for China-ASEAN cooperation, a pragmatic platform for advancing regional economic integration, and a vibrant business card for Guangxi. It has played an important role in serving the construction of a closer China-ASEAN community with a shared future. Trade and investment are key compoments of China and ASEAN cooperation, and promoting China-ASEAN economic and trade cooperation is the original aspirationand mission of the CAEXPO. Over the past 20 years, the CAEXPO platform has brought together a vast array of resources from Chinese and ASEAN enterprises, including goods, services, projects, capital, and information. It has consistently created business opportunities for both sides to explore markets, aiding them in becoming each other's largest trading partners and most active investment collaborators. The Expo has facilitated the implementation of numerous significant mechanisms and projects, propelling the China-ASEAN Free Trade Area from version 1.0 to 2.0 and upgrading to version 3.0.

At present, as the world are undergoing unprecedented changes, the world economy is recovering slowly, international market demand is sluggish, economic globalization is encountering headwinds, and unilateralism and protectionism are on the rise. Under the new circumstances, the CAEXPO has embarked on a new journey of "polishing diamonds into a crown", aiming to upgrade and enhance its platform's functionality. It continues to foster economic growth in the China-ASEAN region and contribute more to building an open global economy. To strengthen the CAEXPO's role as a trade and investment facilitation platform and support the high-quality development of the real economy, the CAEXPO Secretariat has collaborated with Guangxi University to publish the CAEXPO Blue Book - Vision on

China-ASEAN Economic and Trade Cooperation. Starting from 2024, this report will be released annually during the CAEXPO. The book has the following features:

1. **Authority.** The information in this book mainly comes from the relevant government departments of China and ASEAN. It is interpreted, analyzed and predicted by well-known think tanks and industry experts, providing credible views and information support for the business community and academia.

2. **Forward‐looking.** This book not only reviews the China-ASEAN economic and trade cooperation since the last year, and comments on the highlights, key points, characteristics and difficulties, but also provides a forward-looking perspective on the trend of the bilateral economic and trade cooperation. The views put forward are forward-looking, enriching the dimensions for all parties to think about and anticipate trends.

3. **Practicality.** This book is full of detailed content, rich data, typical cases, and strong pertinence. It is suitable for enterprises and researchers engaged in China-Asean economic and trade cooperation to read, and can serve as a reference for decision-making in practical work.

This report is the result of the joint efforts of the China-ASEAN Expo Secretariat, the China-ASEAN Economic School of Guangxi University, the China-ASEAN Research Institute, and other experts. Due to the limited level of the editors, corrections and suggestions are welcome.

Overview

China and ASEAN are good partners who benefit mutually and win together. As an important pillar of the development of bilateral relations, China - ASEAN economic and trade cooperation plays an important role in promoting regional economic growth and building a closer China-ASEAN community with a shared future for mankind. Since 2023, under the strategic guidance of the leaders of China and ASEAN, China and ASEAN have implemented various agreements on the China-ASEAN FTA, and bilateral cooperation in economy and trade has continued to grow, showing strong resilience and vitality. Looking ahead to 2025, bilateral economic and trade cooperation is expected to continue its rapid development momentum.

1 Review of China – ASEAN economic and trade cooperation since 2023

In 2023, China-ASEAN trade in goods, investment cooperation and service trade have achieved new results, and new progress has been made in the negotiations on the 3.0 version of the China-ASEAN FTA.

Firstly , trade in goods remained high. Bilateral trade will reach 911.7 billion U.S. dollars in 2023. In the first half of 2024, bilateral trade reached

US ＄472.45 billion, up by 7.1% year-on-year, ranking first among China's major trading partners in terms of growth rate. The two sides continue to be each other's largest trading partners.

Secondly，mutual investment grew strongly. By the end of 2023, the cumulative mutual investment between China and ASEAN has exceeded 380 billion US dollars. In the first half of 2024, China's direct investment in ASEAN reached US ＄10.75 billion, up 74% year on year. ASEAN's direct investment in China reached US ＄6.46 billion, up 12.9 percent year-on-year. China and ASEAN remain the most active partners in mutual investment.

Thirdly，trade in services expanded at a faster pace. In terms of tourism cooperation, with the support of the visa exemption policy, the number of direct flights between the two sides has reached more than 2,300 per week, and the number of mutual tourist visits between the two sides has recovered rapidly. For example, Thailand received 3.5 million Chinese tourists in 2023, and more than 1.75 million in the first quarter of 2024, making China the first tourist among all countries. Vietnam, Malaysia, Thailand, the Philippines and Singapore are among the top ten source countries (regions) of China's inbound tourism in 2023. In terms of financial cooperation, the amount of bilateral currency swap agreements between China and ASEAN has exceeded 800 billion yuan, and a cross-border RMB clearing network in the ASEAN region has taken shape. In terms of e-commerce cooperation, the China-ASEAN E-commerce Cooperation Development Index was released for the first time, and e-commerce platforms such as Pinduoduo (Temu) have entered ASEAN countries.

Fourthly, negotiations on the 3.0 version of the China−ASEAN FTA were accelerated. Since the launch of the first round of negotiations in 2023, the two sides have exchanged in‐depth views on digital economy, green economy, trade in goods, investment, economic and technical coopera‐ tion, sanitary and phytosanitary measures and other areas, promoted further trade and investment liberalization on the basis of the existing China‐ ASEAN Free Trade Agreement, and expanded practical cooperation in emer‐ ging areas. To build a China‐ASEAN FTA of a higher standard. In June 2024, the 7th round of negotiations was held in Nanning, Guangxi. On the original basis, the two sides substantively completed negotiations on competition and consumer protection, supply chain connectivity, standards technical regulations and conformity assessment procedures.

2　An assessment of China–ASEAN economic and trade coop‐ eration since 2023

Looking back at China‐ASEAN economic and trade cooperation since 2023, the following highlights are observed: **Firstly, the cooperation has strong resilience.** Despite the sluggish world economic recovery, spilt geopolitical influences, increasing trade protection restrictions, and a sharp decline in for‐ eign trade of major economies, China‐ASEAN trade volume has remained at a high level of over 900 billion US dollars. The two sides have actively inves‐ ted in each other, and China's investment in ASEAN in particular has signifi‐ cantly increased. **Secondly, the industrial chain and supply chain have a**

deep integration. In 2023, China's import and export of intermediate goods to ASEAN reached 4.13 trillion-yuan, accounting for 64.4 percent of bilateral trade volume, and ASEAN has remained China's largest trading partner of intermediate goods for many years in a row. **Thirdly, new impetus is emerging.** The "new three" products exported by China to ASEAN, namely green and low-carbon products represented by electric manned vehicles, lithium batteries and solar cells, have grown rapidly. In 2023, Chinese brands will account for 67% of ASEAN NEV sales. Cooperation on clean energy such as wind power, hydropower and solar energy has continued to expand. **Fourthly, further progress was made in institutional opening up.** The two sides have steadily promoted institutional openness and cooperation in the region, including rules, regulations, management and standards. Negotiations on version 3.0 of the China-ASEAN FTA have been accelerated. The Standardization Cooperation and Exchange Center of ASEAN countries has been launched in Nanning. China-Vietnam Friendship Pass-Construction of a friendship Smart port was launched.

At present, there are difficulties in China - ASEAN economic and trade cooperation. **Firstly, the imbalance of trade in goods still exists.** In 2023, China's trade balance with Singapore and Vietnam will both exceed ＄45 billion, and China's trade deficit with Malaysia will exceed ＄15 billion. **Secondly, industrial chain and supply chain cooperation faces challenges.** The backflow of manufacturing in developed countries makes it more difficult for the China-ASEAN manufacturing industry to upgrade the "chain position" in the global industrial chain. **Thirdly, digital economy coopera-**

tion requires further enhancement. The digital economic cooperation between China and ASEAN has insufficient content integrity and accuracy, and it is difficult to unify regional cooperation. **Fourthly, the improvement of economic and trade quality and efficiency needs to break through institutional barriers.** In bilateral economic and trade cooperation, there are still problems such as blocked port logistics, inconvenient cross-border RMB settlement, and inconsistent transportation standards and rules.

3 Prospects for China–ASEAN economic and trade cooperation in 2025

The year 2025 marks the 10th anniversary of the establishment of the ASEAN Community. With the in-depth development of China-ASEAN comprehensive strategic partnership, bilateral economic and trade cooperation is expected to maintain the momentum of rapid development.

Firstly, trade is expected to expand. Our industries are increasingly intertwined. We share common interests in the development of green economy and digital economy. We both attach great importance to economic transformation and upgrading and actively foster new engines of economic growth. Bilateral trade is expected to exceed US $ 1 trillion by 2025. Trade in green products represented by the "new three" will continue to grow, and digital trade will become a new highlight of bilateral cooperation.

Secondly, mutual investment enjoys broad prospects. Asean countries' demand for infrastructure construction in transportation, energy, communications and other fields continues to expand, providing huge business opportunities for investment cooperation between the two sides. The restructuring of the global industrial chain will make the industrial chain and supply chain cooperation between the two sides closer, and promote the investment cooperation between the two sides in their respective advantageous industries and their upstream and downstream industries. For example, China's Geely Auto, building on the success of its joint venture with Malaysia's Proton Motors, plans to invest another $ 10 billion to build a car manufacturing center in Tanjung Malim, Malaysia.

Thirdly, the quality of trade in services has increased. With the gradual resumption of more international flights and the implementation of the visa waiver policy, tourism cooperation between the two sides is expected to return to the pre-epidemic level. The construction of the Pinglu Canal, the backbone of a new international land-sea trade corridor, will be accelerated, the functions of the Beibu Gulf international gateway port will continue to improve, and China-ASEAN multimodal transport cooperation will continue to strengthen, which will promote bilateral cooperation in ports, railways and other international transport services. The steady expansion of institutional openness and cooperation in rules, regulations, management and standards between China and ASEAN will deepen trade in services such as finance, digital trade, software maintenance and international education.

Fourthly, the 3.0 version of the FTZ has been effective. With the conclusion of negotiations on version 3.0 of the China-ASEAN FTA, the level of trade and investment liberalization in the region has been further upgraded, practical cooperation in emerging areas such as digital economy and green economy has been expanded, and a more inclusive, modern, comprehensive and mutually beneficial China-ASEAN Free Trade Area has been formed. The 22nd China-ASEAN Expo to be held in 2025 will strive to promote the effective implementation of the 3.0 version of the China-ASEAN FTA, so that enterprises on both sides can share the benefits brought by the high-level free trade area and the fruits of the building of the China-ASEAN community of common destiny.

Ⅰ China—ASEAN economic and trade cooperation since 2023

In 2023, China-ASEAN economic and trade cooperation has experienced rapid development. Trade in goods has remained at a high level, investment cooperation has remained strong, trade in services has been opened wider, and negotiations on the version 3.0 of the China-ASEAN FTA have accelerated.

1.1 Trade in goods remained at a high level

1.1.1 Scale. The total trade in goods between China and ASEAN in 2023 fell slightly from 2022 to 911.472 billion US dollars, a decrease of 4.9% compared with 2022. Among them, China's imports from ASEAN reached 387.924 billion US dollars, down 4.8% year on year. The trade volume of goods exported from China to ASEAN in 2023 was 551.046 billion US dollars, down 27.498 billion US dollars from 2022.

1.1.2 Commodity structure. The "new three" products that China exports to ASEAN are green and low-carbon products represented by electric manned vehicles, lithium batteries and solar cells, and the growth in 2022 and 2023 is becoming the highlight of China-ASEAN trade in goods. In

2022, China's exports of "new three" products to ASEAN grew strongly, and exports exceeded 11 billion US dollars for the first time in 2023.

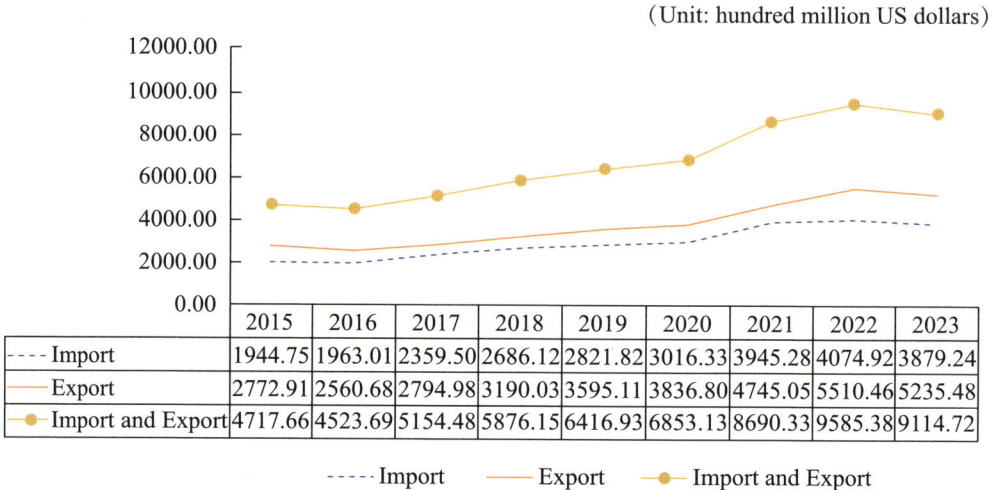

（Unit: hundred million US dollars）

	2015	2016	2017	2018	2019	2020	2021	2022	2023
----Import	1944.75	1963.01	2359.50	2686.12	2821.82	3016.33	3945.28	4074.92	3879.24
—— Export	2772.91	2560.68	2794.98	3190.03	3595.11	3836.80	4745.05	5510.46	5235.48
—●— Import and Export	4717.66	4523.69	5154.48	5876.15	6416.93	6853.13	8690.33	9585.38	9114.72

----- Import —— Export —●— Import and Export

Figure 1 Trade of goods between China and ASEAN，2015—2023

Source: General Administration of Customs, the People's Republic of China

Table 1 Trade volume and growth rate of China–ASEAN

"New three" products from 2021 to 2023

Years	Imports （Thousands of US dollars）	Exports （Thousands of US dollars）	Imports and Exports （Thousands of US dollars）	Growth rate （%）
2021	1535381.91	5685844.16	7221226.08	—
2022	2676201.97	8206394.42	10882596.39	50.70%
2023	1362423.44	11464593.93	12827017.37	17.87%

Source: General Administration of Customs, the People's Republic of China

1.1.3 Country structure. In 2023, the top three countries in the trade volume of goods between China and ASEAN are Vietnam, Malaysia and

Indonesia, and whether it is import or export, the top two are Vietnam and Malaysia, which shows that the two countries are China's main trading partners in ASEAN.

Table 2　The trade volume of goods between China and ASEAN countries in 2023 and ranking

Ranking	Country	Imports and Exports (Thousands of US dollars)
1	Vietnam	229793472.77
2	Malaysia	190243547.63
3	Indonesia	139415895.91
4	Thailand	126279946.13
5	Singapore	108393419.38
6	Philippines	71909581.03
7	Myanmar	20949404.81
8	Cambodia	14822297.93
9	Laos	7102232.58
10	Brunei	2804681.89

Source: General Administration of Customs, the People's Republic of China

1.1.4 Trade balance. In 2023, China's trade partners with a trade surplus are Myanmar, the Philippines, Singapore, Thailand, Vietnam and Cambodia, while its trade partners with a trade deficit are Indonesia, Malaysia, Brunei and Laos.

Table 3 Balance of trade in goods between China and ASEAN countries in 2023

Country	Exports (Thousands of US dollars)	Imports (Thousands of US dollars)	Balance of trade (Thousands of US dollars)
Myanmar	11401673.88	9547730.90	1853942.98
Indonesia	65200435.56	74215460. 00	-9015024.44
Malaysia	87382851.94	102860696. 00	-15477844.06
Philippines	52413350.81	19496230. 00	32917120.81
Singapore	76963629.70	31429790. 00	45533839.70
Thailand	75736059.56	50543887. 00	25192172.56
Vietnam	137611635. 00	92181838. 00	45429797.00
Brunei	857608.11	1947073.80	-1089465.69
Laos	3348297.04	3753935.50	-405638.46
Cambodia	12752000.75	2070297.20	10681703.55

Source: General Administration of Customs, People's Republic of China

1.2 Two–way investment grew strongly

1.2.1 Scale. In 2023, China's direct investment in ASEAN reached 17.306 billion US dollars, ranking fourth among ASEAN's sources of foreign investment, accounting for 7.50% of ASEAN's total foreign investment and 11.71% of China's outward foreign direct investment. In 2022, ASEAN's investment in China reached a new high, with the investment scale increasing by 12.58% year-on-year to reach 11.908 billion US dollars. ASEAN is the second largest source of foreign investment in China, accounting for 6.29% of China's actual utilization of foreign investment.

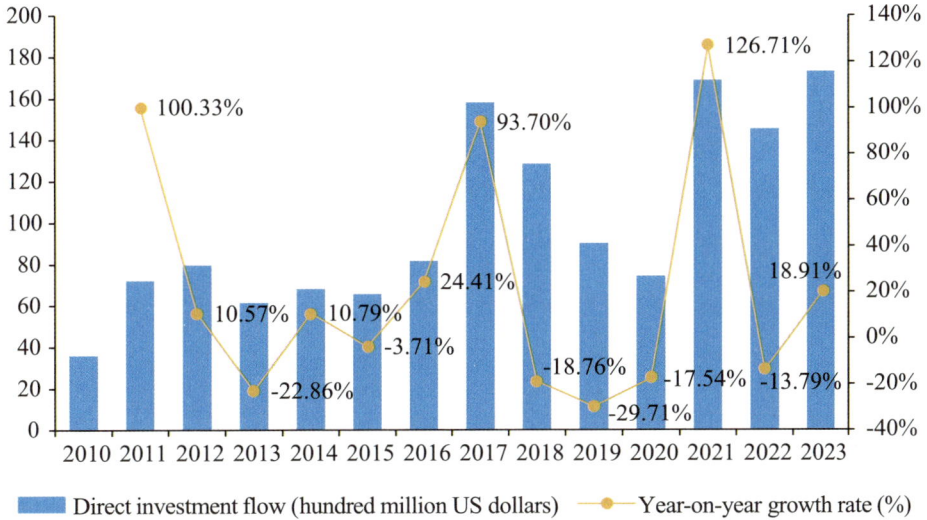

Figure 2　Scale and growth rate of China's direct investment in ASEAN, 2010—2023

Source: The ASEAN Secretariat, Ministry of Commerce of the People's Republic of China

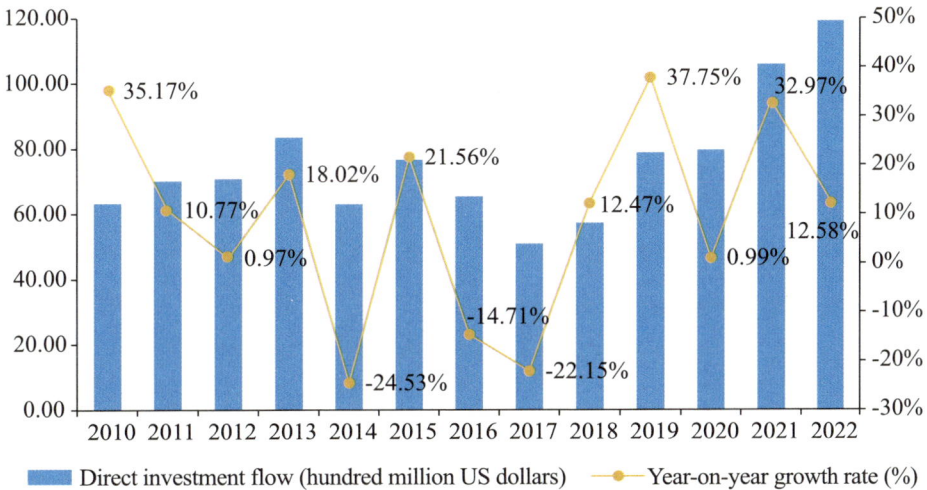

Figure 3　Scale and growth rate of ASEAN direct investment in China, 2010—2022

Source: National Bureau of Statistics of China

1.2.2 Industry distribution. In 2023, China's direct investment in ASEAN is mainly concentrated in manufacturing, wholesale and retail trade, motor vehicle and motorcycle repair, real estate and other industries. Among them, the investment in manufacturing industry was 6.253 billion US dollars, up 11.63% year on year; Wholesale and retail trade, motor vehicles and motorcycle repair investment of 3.616 billion US dollars, an increase of 77.12%; The investment in the real estate industry reached 3.212 billion US dollars, up 42.51% year on year.

Table 4　Industry distribution of China's FDI to ASEAN in 2022 and 2023

Industry	2022		2023	
	Flow (Million US dollar)	Proportion (%)	Flow (Million US dollar)	Proportion (%)
Agriculture, forestry and fishery	76.9	0.5	79.8	0.5
Mining industry	61.6	0.4	146.4	0.8
Manufacturing industry	5,602.0	38.5	6, 253.3	36.1
Electricity, gas, steam and air conditioning supply	425.5	2.9	837.6	4.8
Water supply; Wastewater treatment, waste management and remediation activities	-1.7	0.0	-10.8	-0.1
construction industry	605.6	4.2	696.2	4.0
Wholesale and retail trade; Motor vehicle and motorcycle repair	2,041.6	14.0	3,616.1	20.9
Transportation and storage	498.7	3.4	465.6	2.7
hotel and catering sectors	82.9	0.6	67.0	0.4

continued

Industry	2022		2023	
	Flow (Million US dollar)	Proportion (%)	Flow (Million US dollar)	Proportion (%)
Information and communication industry	260.4	1.8	182.4	1.1
Finance and insurance industry	2, 169.7	14.9	1,401.9	8.1
Professional and scientific activities	61.1	0.4	-102.4	-0.6
Business management and business services	-3.9	0.0	14.0	0.1
Public administration and defence; Mandatory social security	0.0	0.0	5.3	0.0
Education	22.3	0.2	1.0	0.0
Health and social welfare	0.2	0.0	23.5	0.1
Arts, entertainment and recreational activities	-1.7	0.0	-0.3	0.0
Other service activities	398.6	2.7	416.9	2.4
Other industries	0.0	0.0	0.0	0.0
Total	14,553.6	100.0	17,305.7	100.0

Source: ASEAN Statistics Division

1.2.3 Country structure. China's direct investment in ASEAN in 2023 goes mainly to Singapore, Vietnam, Indonesia and Cambodia. From the perspective of ASEAN's direct investment in China, Singapore occupies an absolute leading position, accounting for more than 90% of ASEAN's direct investment in China on average from 2020 to 2022.

Table 5   Country structure of Chinaś FDI to ASEAN from 2021 to 2023

Country	2021		2022		2023	
	Flow (Million US dollar)	Proportion (%)	Flow (Million US dollar)	Proportion (%)	Flow (Million US dollar)	Proportion (%)
Singapore	6532.30	38.69	5825.60	40.03	7152.00	41.33
Other	2207.19	13.07	2017.23	13.86	3412.63	19.72
Cambodia	1176.51	6.97	1508.40	10.36	1991.41	11.51
Indonesia	5075.71	30.06	3510.51	24.12	1674.47	9.68
Thailand	1361.96	8.07	945.91	6.50	1567.53	9.06
Malaysia	495.57	2.94	837.50	5.75	889.49	5.14
Myanmar	15.25	0.09	-107.26	-0.74	602.14	3.48
Philippines	18.53	0.11	15.69	0.11	15.99	0.09
Total	16883.01	100	14553.58	100	17305.66	100

Source: The ASEAN Secretariat

1.3   Trade in services expanded at a faster pace

In 2001, the construction process of the China ASEAN Free Trade Area was launched, and the two sides signed the Agreement on Trade in Services in 2007, in which countries reached the first batch of service market-opening commitments in the form of positive lists and made specific opening commitments for various sectors of service trade. The service trade barriers between China and ASEAN have been lowered, and the scale of bilateral service trade has grown rapidly, from 18.695 billion US dollars in 2007 to 32.402 billion US dollars in 2011, with an average annual growth rate of 19.09%. In 2011, based on the first batch of specific commitments, China and ASEAN signed the second batch of specific commitments on service trade opening, and further opened the service trade market based on the first batch of commitments on service trade opening. The breadth and depth of the opening up of the second batch of China-ASEAN service trade commitments have significantly improved, and service trade barriers between China and ASEAN have been greatly lowered. The scale of bilateral service trade has increased from 32.402 billion US dollars in 2011 to 72.666 billion US dollars in 2021, with an average annual growth rate of 9.95%. In 2022, the RCEP Agreement officially came into force, promising further opening up of service trade in the form of a negative list, and ushering in the new development of China-ASEAN service trade.

Owing to the lag in the update of the bilateral service trade data, the latest data are only updated until 2021.Combined with the data on China-ASEAN foreign service trade, the development of China-ASEAN service trade shows the following characteristics.

1.3.1 Scale. The scale of trade in services between China and ASEAN countries has grown rapidly, showing great vitality and potential for development. In 2023, China's service trade volume will reach 933.1 billion US dollars, up 4.95% year-on-year; The scale of ASEAN's service trade reached 1,057.653 billion US dollars, up 6.66% year-on-year. The scale of service trade in ASEAN countries has grown rapidly, and the potential for service trade is huge. According to data from 2007 to 2023, the average annual growth rate of China's service trade is 10.04%, and the average annual growth rate of ASEAN's service trade is 8.58%, much higher than the average annual growth rate of world service trade of 5.94%. Foreign service trade between China and ASEAN has shown great vitality.

The scale of China-ASEAN two-way service trade is expanding daily, and China and ASEAN are important partners in service trade. As shown in Figure 4, from 2010 to 2021, the scale of China-ASEAN bilateral service trade expanded from 27.01 billion US dollars to 72.666 billion US dollars, an increase of 269% and an average annual growth rate of 9.95%. Among them, China's imports from ASEAN rose from 15.048 billion US dollars to 39.294 billion US dollars, up 261%, with an annual growth rate of 9.84%. Exports to ASEAN rose from 11.962 billion US dollars to 33.372 billion US dollars, an increase of 279%, with an annual growth rate of 10.17%.

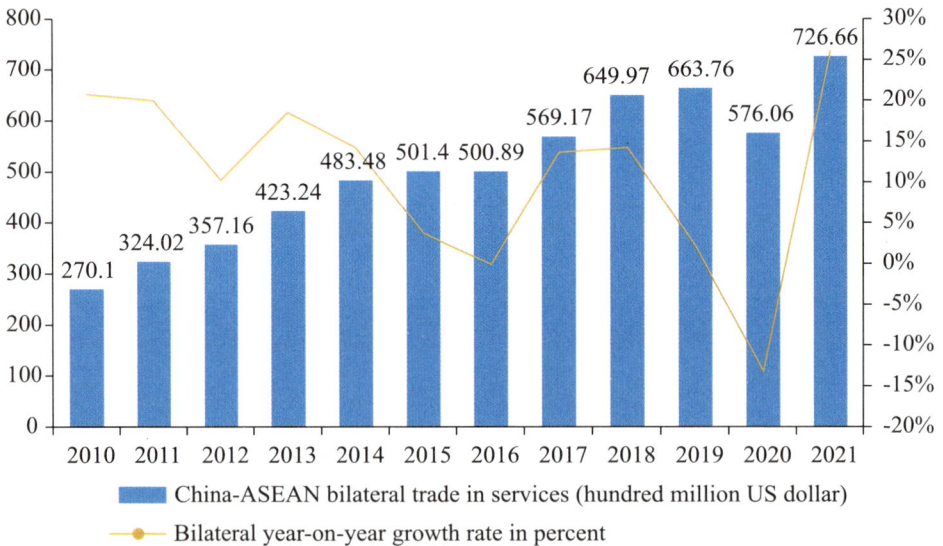

Figure 4   Scale of China–ASEAN bilateral service trade, 2010—2021

Source: WTO Stats

It can be seen from Table 6 that China's import and export of service trade with ASEAN countries were basically in deficit, and the deficithas expanded before the epidemic, but it narrowed sharply after the epidemic. In 2021, the scale of China's export to ASEAN reached 33.372 billion US dollars, up 25. 25% year-on-year, accounting for 11.22% of China's export of service trade in the same period. In the same year, China's service trade volume from ASEAN countries reached 39.294 billion US dollars, up 26.14% year-on-year, accounting for 10.87% of China's total foreign service import in the same period. From 2011 to 2021, the scale of China's service trade imports from ASEAN showed an upward trend, with the average annual growth rate of China's service trade imports from ASEAN reaching 9.84%, higher than the growth rate of world service trade imports. It declined briefly in 2020 due to the impact of the epidemic and recovered to pre-epidemic levels in 2021.

Table 6   China's import and export of service trade to ASEAN from 2010 to 2021

Years	Exports (hundred million US dollars)	Imports (hundred million US dollars)	Trade balance (hundred million US dollars)
2010	119.62	150.48	-30.86
2011	144.41	179.61	-35.2
2012	157.75	199.41	-41.66
2013	191.43	231.81	-40.38
2014	215.99	267.49	-51.5
2015	217.49	283.91	-66.42
2016	215.25	285.64	-70.39
2017	242.68	326.49	-83.81

continued

Years	Exports (hundred million US dollars)	Imports (hundred million US dollars)	Trade balance (hundred million US dollars)
2018	265.89	384.08	-118.19
2019	280	383.76	-103.76
2020	266.44	309.62	-43.18
2021	333.72	392.94	-59.22

Source: WTO Stats

1.3.2 Sector structure. The service industry in China and ASEAN has similarities and complementarities. Service trade between the two sides is still dominated by the traditional service sector. In recent years, the share of trade in the emerging service sector has been rising and the proportion has been increasing, which has a huge development space and potential.

As shown in Figures 5 and 6 that in terms of exports, China's exports to ASEAN are concentrated in traditional sectors such as transportation, other business services and tourism. The scale and proportion of exports of telecommunications, computer and information technology services have been increasing, while the proportion of exports of financial services has been increasing, but the scale is limited. In 2019, China's export of service trade to ASEAN reached 28 billion US dollars, concentrated in four sectors: transportation, other business services, tourism and construction, which together accounted for more than 80 percent of China's total export of service trade to ASEAN. Affected by the epidemic, China's export of service trade to ASEAN declined slightly in 2020 and recovered to the pre-epidemic level by 2021. In 2021, China's export of service trade to ASEAN reached 33.377 billion US dollars, up 25.25% year-on-year, concentrated in four sectors: transport, other business services, construction, telecommunications, computers and information services. This accounts for 38.10%, 24.73%, 13.43% and 10.06% respectively. Owing to the impact of the epidemic, the world's tourism service exports have shrunk significantly. China's tourism service trade exports to ASEAN have also decreased from 17.99% in 2019 to 3.65% in 2021, while the proportion of the transportation sector has risen rapidly.

(Unit: hundred million US dollars)

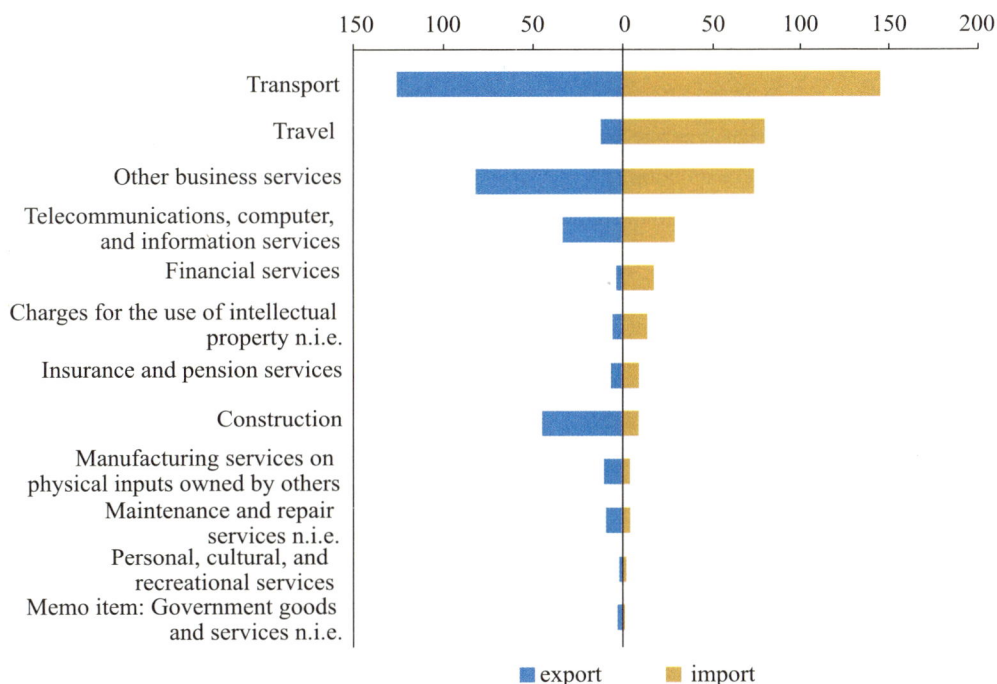

Figure 5   China's service trade import and export to ASEAN by sector in 2021

Source: WTO Stats

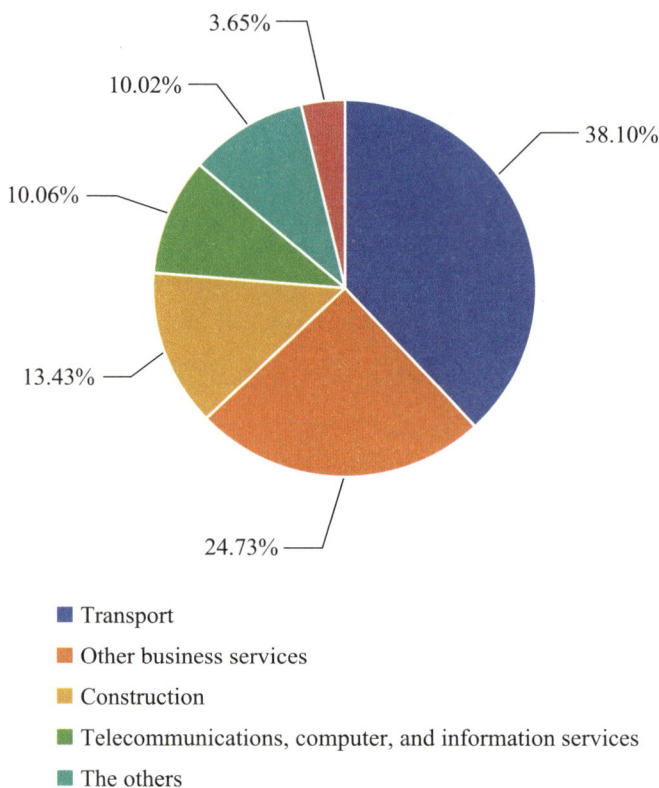

Figure 6   China's services trade exports to ASEAN by Sector in 2021

Source: WTO Stats

It can be seen from Figure 5 and Figure 7 that in terms of imports, ASEAN's export services to China are mainly concentrated in tourism, transportation and other business service sectors. Affected by the epidemic, ASEAN tourism service exports have suffered a serious setback. The proportion of ASEAN countries' tourism service exports to China has decreased from 52. 91% in 2019 to 20.27% in 2021. Meanwhile, the scale of service trade exports from the transport sector to China has expanded rapidly. Rose to 14. 522 billion US dollars in 2021 from 8.832 billion US dollars in 2019. Exports of other business services jumped 62.59 percent from a year earlier to USD 7,416 million. In terms of specific countries, Singapore is an important source country of China's import of service trade. In 2021, the total export of service trade to China reached 23.774 billion US dollars, accounting for 60.50% of the total export of ASEAN countries to China, making it the fourth largest source country or region of China's import of service trade, mainly transport service export. The service trade exports of Thailand, Malaysia, Vietnam and the Philippines to China are concentrated in the tourism sector, which is sluggish after the epidemic, and the proportion of service trade exports also decreases accordingly.

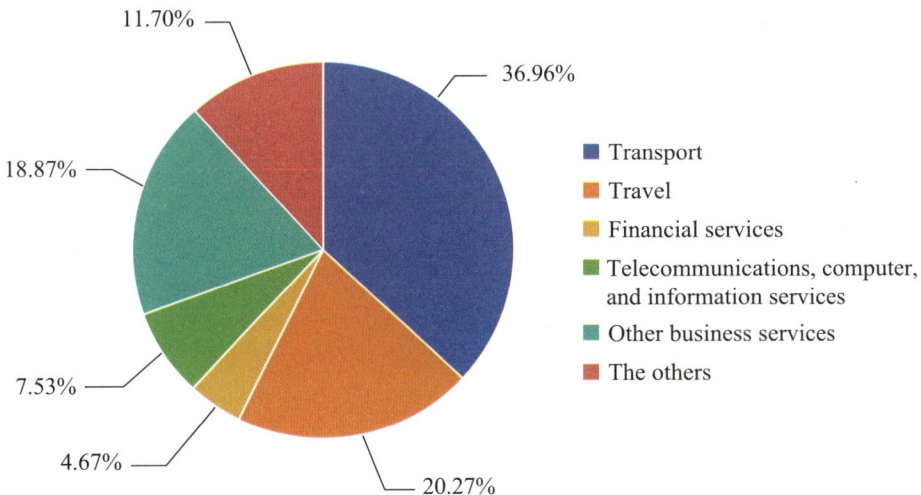

Figure 7　China's service trade imports from ASEAN by Sector in 2021

Source: WTO Stats

1.3.3 Country structure. It can be seen from Table 7 that China's import and export of service trade to ASEAN countries are relatively concentrated, mainly Singapore, Thailand, the Philippines and Vietnam. Singapore accounted for the highest proportion. In 2021, China's exports to Singapore reached 15.978 billion US dollars, and its imports reached 23.734 billion US dollars, making it the third largest trade destination for China's service trade exports, after Hong Kong China and the United States. In terms of imports and exports, China's imports and exports to ASEAN countries show different characteristics.

In terms of exports, the scale of China's service trade exports to ASEAN continues to grow, but the proportion of different countries in the region is extremely unbalanced. China's service trade exports to ASEAN are mainly concentrated in Singapore, Thailand, Malaysia and Vietnam, accounting for 47.88%, 13.09%, 11.85% and 11.20% respectively. And after the epidemic, the proportion of Singapore and Vietnam increased, while the proportion of Malaysia decreased. This is because China's service trade exports to Singapore are mainly concentrated in three sectors, namely transportation, other business services, telecommunications, and computer and information services, which were less affected by the pandemic; Vietnam has undertaken industrial transfer from China and developed countries, and has a large demand for infrastructure and manufacturing services. Service trade exports to Vietnam, Malaysia, Thailand and other countries grew rapidly. Affected by the epidemic, China's export of tourism services to Thailand and Malaysia has declined rapidly, while the proportion of transportation services has increased significantly. China's export volume of service trade to Indonesia, the Philippines, Myanmar, Cambodia, Brunei, Laos and other ASEAN countries shows an increasing trend, but the export scale is still small and concentrated in transportation, construction, other business services and other sectors.

In terms of imports, Singapore is an important source country of China's service trade imports. In 2021, Singapore's total service trade exports to China reached 23.774 billion US dollars, accounting for 60.50% of ASEAN countries' total exports to China, making it the fourth largest source country or region of China's service trade imports. The service trade exports of Thailand, Malaysia, Vietnam and the Philippines to China are concentrated in the tourism sector, which is sluggish after the epidemic, and the proportion of service trade exports also decreases accordingly.

Table 7 China's import and export of service trade to the ten ASEAN countries in 2021

Country	Exports (hundred million US dollars)	Imports (hundred million US dollars)
Singapore	159.78	237.74
Thailand	43.7	43.61
Philippines	39.55	30.64
Vietnam	37.38	27.14
Indonesia	28.63	23.79
Malaysia	16.61	21.63
Myanmar	2.99	4.6
Laos	2.33	2.03
Cambodia	1.94	1.23
Brunei	0.81	0.53

Source: WTO Stats

1.4　Negotiations on the 3.0 version of the China–ASEAN FTA have been accelerated

The establishment and development of China - ASEAN Free Trade Area (CAFTA) is an important strategic choice made jointly by China and ASEAN countries in order to cope with global economic changes and foster their own economic development under the background of global economic integration. The establishment of CAFTA has not only promoted the significant enhancement of economic and trade exchanges between the two sides, enhanced the overall strength and influence of the regional economy, but also provided a successful model of economic integration and regional cooperation for other developing countries in the world.

Since the 1990s, global economic integration hasbeen accelerating , and regional economic cooperation has become an important way for countries to enhance their competitiveness. The outbreak of the Asian financial crisis has further highlighted the importance of strengthening regional cooperation and enhancing the ability of economy to resist risks, which has accelerated the process of CAFTA. In addition, China has shown a high sense of responsibility and an open stance in the WTO, which has laid a solid foundation for the establishment of CAFTA. In this context, China and ASEAN countries began to explore the possibility of establishing a free trade area based on their common development needs and geographical advantages.

1.4.1　Implementation effect of CAFTA version 1.0

In 2002, China and ASEAN signed theFramework Agreement on China -

ASEAN Comprehensive Economic Cooperation and launched the construction of the free trade area. This cooperation encompasses trade in goods, services, and investment. Since the signing of the Agreement on Trade in Goods in 2004, countries within the region have significantly lowered tariff barriers and promoted the circulation of commodities. By 2018, two-way trade between China and ASEAN had reached US ＄587.87 billion, an increase of nearly 10 times compared with that before the signing of the Framework Agreement. Since the signing of the Agreement on Trade in Services in 2007, the two sides have continuously deepened cooperation in the field of services, and the volume of service trade has increased significantly. In 2018, the total volume of bilateral service trade reached US ＄58.45 billion, an increase of 227.7% compared with the year of the signing of the agreement. Since the signing of the Investment Agreement in 2009, two-way investment has continued to grow. From 2010 to 2018, China's investment in ASEAN increased from US ＄7.3 billion to over US ＄11 billion, reaching a peak of US ＄13.62 billion in 2017. In general, the economic and trade cooperation between China and ASEAN has strong moment and it is necessary to continuously strengthen cooperation and build a more stable and efficient economic relationship.

1.4.2　Implementation effect of CAFTA version 2.0

On November 22, 2015, the Protocol on Upgrading the CAFTA was formally signed and took full effect for all members on October 22, 2019, forming the CAFTA Version 2.0.

In the field of goods trade, the CAFTA version 2.0 focuses on rules of origin and trade facilitation measures. In terms of rules of origin, the threshold for goods to obtain origin qualification has been lowered, and more accurate formats and labeling methods have been combined to improve the efficiency of enterprise customs declaration. In terms of trade facilitation, the two sides have reduced the time and cost of customs clearance for enterprises by optimizing customs procedures. The total bilateral trade between China and ASEAN have increased from 4.43 trillion yuan in 2019 to 6.41 trillion yuan in 2023, with a growth rate of 44.70 percent.

In the field of service trade and investment, China has made improvement commitments in many industries, and ASEAN countries have made higher-level opening-up commitments to China in about 70 sub-sectors in eight areas. In terms of technical and economic cooperation, the two sides agreed to expand more than 10 areasbeyond the existing scope and provide financial support for related projects.

1.4.3　Reasons for CAFTA 3.0 upgrade

First, the potential of two-way trade and investment should be further stimulated. From 2010 to 2023, the economic and trade relations between China and ASEAN showed a high level of development and strong development potential. Over the 13-year period, the average annual growth rate of trade volume was 11.54%, about 3.5 percentage points higher than the average growth rate of China's import and export. The proportion of China-ASEAN import and export in China increased from 9.85% to 15.36%. The status of China's trade with ASEAN in the national economy is constantly improving. At the same time, the proportion of trade in high value-added products between China and ASEAN has been increasing, and trade in services has expanded significantly. Against the background of many uncertainties and challenges in the current world economic environment, it is particularly important to upgrade the free trade area to further enhance the resilience and stability of economic cooperation, expand the areas and depth of cooperation, and find new economic growth points.

Second, regional economic integration should be promoted to address global challenges. At a time when global economic growth is slowing down and trade protectionism is on the rise, China and ASEAN must continue to enhance regional economic cooperation if they are to maintain sustained and high- quality regional economic cooperation. The upgrade of the CAFTA version 3. 0 will form a closer community with a shared future, promote the construction of larger economic integration, and provide a stable external environment for regional development. The upgrade of the free trade area will enable the two sides to reach consensus on more issues, participate in international affairs with a greater voice, and take a greater initiative in global development.

Third, the challenge of multilateral economic and trade agreements at higher levels. With the signing and implementation of multilateral trade agreements, the CAFTA not only has the potential of sustainable development, but also faces the possibility of dilution. In the context of the formal implementation of RCEP, the original FTA agreements have a backward trend. The RCEP agreement demonstrates the firm determination of both sides to promote regional economic integration and the pursuit of common interests. Coupled with a more perfect system of rules, it has made an important reference for the future development direction of CAFTA. To sum up, the formal implementation of RCEP provides a practical basis and power source for the upgrading of CAFTA version 3.0, which is an inevitable choice.

Fourth, it is imperative to cultivate new engines of economic growth and to share new development opportunities. The leap in information technology has propelled the digital economy as a new engine of global economic growth, which is quite different from traditional trade. However, there is a large gap in the level of digital economy among the members of the free trade area, and there are gaps in the relevant rules of the agreement, which leads to conflicts and uncertainties in the cooperation of the two sides in the digital economy. Therefore, it is urgent to carry out "upgraded" negotiations on the CAFTA.

Green economy has become an important driving force for economic growth. First of all, joining the green economy related rules can further reduce the tariff level between China and ASEAN countries, while breaking down the relevant non-tariff barriers and realizing the upgrading of trade liberalization. Second, enhancing trade facilitation can be achieved by bolstering regional cooperation on green infrastructure. Finally, China and ASEAN countries can take the opportunity of negotiation to carry out more cooperation in relevant aspects and stimulate the vitality of technological innovation in the region.

Fifth, the upgrading of the CAFTA has benefited enterprises and people. At the enterprise level, upgrading brings about a stable economic and trade environment and reduces policy uncertainty. In terms of investment, the scope of investment has been expanded, the level of rights and interests protection has been improved, and industrial cooperation has been strengthened. At the same time, the upgrading of the free trade zone will help enterprises take advantage of new drivers such as the digital economy and enhance their competitive advantages. In addition, CAFTA version 3.0 is also expected to facilitate the personnel mobility and help enterprises operate across borders. At the people's level, with the upgrading of the FTZ rules and the accelerated flow of high-quality products within the region, consumers will have more opportunities to choose high-quality products and meet more diversified needs. In addition, the upgrade of FTZ rules will drive the development of more industries andgenerate more employment opportunities, especially in areas such as digital technology and green economy.

1.4.4   CAFTA 3.0 negotiation outlook

Trade in goods. In terms of tariffs, it will raise the level of tariff reduction and reduce non-tariff barriers. In terms of rules of origin, it will adopt more simplified and flexible standards of origin; improve the level of facilitation of Certificate of Origin application; and strengthen linkage with other multilateral trade agreements and improve the consistency of rules. In terms of trade facilitation, it will simplify procedures, reduce compliance costs and speeds up the release of goods; accelerate the construction of standardized infrastructure to improve the efficiency and safety of cargo transportation; carry out the digital construction of ports and accelerate the application of information technology in trade.

E-commerce. Firstly, enhance e-commerce trade facilitation by accepting electronic document formats and establishing unified standards for electronic authentication and signatures. Secondly, improve the business environment, strengthen information protection and protect the rights and interests of consumers. Thirdly, build an integrated and comprehensive cross - border e-commerce platform, realize the docking of various functional departments, and accelerate data sharing and process optimization.

Digital economy cooperation. Promote cross-border data flow on the basis of strengthening digital infrastructure by benchmarking high-standard economic and trade rules such as the RCEP; explore new models and forms of business for technology application by accelerating the combination of digital technology application and trade; further promote trade in digital services and accelerate the export of relevant digital content; strengthen the protection of digital intellectual property rights and the training of talents to enhance the innovation capacity and the healthy development of digital industries in the region.

Green economy cooperation. Both sides should enhance the green level of industries on the basis of strengthening the sharing and cooperation of green technologies; accelerate the establishment of green standards and certification systems to make standards more scientific and operational. In terms of finance, special green investment and financing mechanisms and new tools will be established to provide guarantee for green projects; in addition, the two sides will also clarify the goals and responsibilities, and form a coordinated regional low-carbon development pattern through jointly formulating carbon neutrality action plans and carbon trading markets.

Supply chain connectivity. Release a new master plan for connectivity to upgrade supply chain infrastructure construction; continue to accelerate the digitalization and green construction of relevant infrastructure and supply chain, improve the transparency, traceability and intelligence level of supply chain, and achieve the sustainable development of supply chain; strengthen supply chain risk management and enhance supply chain resilience by establishing emergency response mechanisms and risk early warning systems.

Preferential policies for small and medium-sized enterprises. Firstly, training on the rules of the free trade zone will be carried out for small and medium-sized enterprises to improve their coping ability and market competitiveness. Secondly, the administrative restrictions of the government should be reduced to ensure that smes enjoy fair treatment in the markets within and outside the region, and discriminatory practices should be prohibited. In terms of financial support, exclusive credit policies will be introduced, and big data and other technological means will be used to reduce financing costs. In terms of legal protection, legal exchanges within the region will be strengthened, necessary legal aid services will be provided to SMEs, and the legal awareness of enterprises will be enhanced to safeguard the free competition of SMEs.

II Review on China–ASEAN economic and trade cooperation since 2023

Examining the China-ASEAN economic and trade cooperation since 2023, several highlights emerge: first, the partnership has demonstrated remarkable resilience; second, there has been a profound interweaving of industrial and supply chain networks; third, new driving forces for growth have emerged; fourth, there have been advancements in institutional opening-up. Currently, the focal points of China-ASEAN economic and trade cooperation are to deepen and strengthen connectivity, integrate the digital economy, and foster green, low-carbon and high-quality development. However, several challenges persist: the imbalance in goods trade remains, industrial and supply chain cooperation encounters challenges, digital economic cooperation requires further enhancement, and the improvement of economic and trade quality and efficiency need to overcome institutional barriers.

2.1 Highlights of China–ASEAN economic and trade cooperation

2.1.1 Strong resilience of cooperation

Trade and investment cooperation grew steadily. In terms of trade, despite the weak recovery of the world economy, spillover of geopolitical effects, increasing trade protection restrictions and a sharp decline in foreign trade of major economies, China-ASEAN bilateral trade has remained at a high level of over US $ 900 billion. In 2023, China and ASEAN will be each other's largest trading partner for the fourth consecutive year. In terms of investment, the two sides have actively invested in each other, and the scale of China's investment in ASEAN has increased significantly. In 2023, China's investment in ASEAN will increase by up to 44.6 percent, with two-way cumulative investment exceeding 380 billion US dollars. ASEAN has become the most concentrated area for Chinese auto companies to invest overseas. Chinese brands accounts for 67 percent of new energy vehicle sales in ASEAN in 2023. The Greater Bay Area and Hainan Free Trade Port have achieved initial significant results in cooperation with ASEAN, and the Southeast Asia Investment Center of Hainan Free Trade Port has been officially put into operation. China has set up more than 6,500 enterprises with direct investment in ASEAN. Relying on the "two countries and two Parks", the two sides have jointly built demonstration parks for economic and trade innovation and development, opening up a new channel for ASEAN countries to integrate into China's local opening-up and development.

Regional economic integration is deepening. The deepening of China-ASEAN economic and trade cooperation cannot be separated from the institutional support of free trade agreement. Negotiations on upgrading the CAFTA version 3.0 are progressing in an orderly manner, and seven rounds of consultations have been held. China and all ASEAN parties will work together to build a higher-level free trade area. Meanwhile, more than two years after the Regional Comprehensive Economic Partnership (RCEP) came into force, regional trade costs have been significantly reduced, production and supply chains have been more closely linked, and tangible benefits have been brought to member states.[1]

Development assistance cooperation has been strengthened. China has given priority to providing economic and technical assistance to Cambodia, Laos, Myanmar and Vietnam to support ASEAN in narrowing the internal development gap and promoting integrated development, including supporting ASEAN countries in building infrastructure projects to boost economic and social development. We will carry out cooperation on poverty reduction, health and disaster relief projects to improve people's well-being in ASEAN countries. Through scholarships, short-term training and other human resource development programs, we will help ASEAN countries cultivate talents in various fields and enhance their capacity for independent development.

2.1.2　Deep integration of industrial and supply chains

In 2023, in terms of import and export of intermediate goods, the trade volume between China and ASEAN countries will reach 4.13 trillion yuan, accounting for 64.4% of the total bilateral trade, and ASEAN has been Chi-

---

[1]　Foreign ministry web site. China to asean investment growth in 2023 is as high as 44.6% [EB/OL], 2024-07-27. https://investgo.cn/article/yw/ tzyj / 202407/732344. HTML. Read the date: 30 July 2024.

na's largest trading partner for intermediate goods for many consecutive years.[①]The two-way investment model of China-ASEAN industrial chain and supply chain has been further developed, which is reflected in the following aspects: first, trade relations. The two-way investment model has promoted bilateral cooperation in manufacturing, agriculture, service and other fields, improved the level of trade facilitation, reduced trade costs, and thus increased bilateral trade volume. For example, Chinese enterprises invest in infrastructure construction in ASEAN countries, which drives the export of related equipment and technology, and agricultural products and raw materials from ASEAN countries are exported to China, which meets China's market demand. Second, investment structure. The two-way investment mode makes the investment structure of both sides more diversified and improves the investment efficiency. China's investment in ASEAN countries mainly focuses on infrastructure construction, real estate and manufacturing, while ASEAN countries' investment in China mainly focuses on manufacturing, service and science and technology. This complementary investment structure is conducive to the coordinated economic development of both sides. Third, peace and stability. The two-way investment model will help enhance mutual understanding and trust between the two sides, reduce geopolitical risks and safeguard regional peace and stability. Through economic cooperation, the national interests of both sides are more closely

---

① Economic observation network. How to keep the foreign trade toughness [EB/OL]. (2024-08-03) [2024-01-16]. https://www.163.com/dy/article/ IOILP8B605118O92. HTML.

linked, which helps to resolve disputes through dialogue and cooperation. For example, the model of two-way investment cooperation between China and ASEAN countries is Singapore, which is the largest investment destination of China in ASEAN countries and the largest source of investment of ASEAN countries in China. The two sides have carried out extensive cooperation in finance, logistics, science and technology, and jointly promoted the development of bilateral trade. This two-way investment model not only promotes the economic development of the two sides, but also helps to enhance the cooperation between the two sides in international affairs and jointly safeguard regional peace and stability.[1]

2.1.3 New emerging impetus for cooperation

First, the scale of trade in new energy products has expanded. The "new three" products that China exports to ASEAN, namely green and low-carbon products represented by electric passenger vehicles, lithium batteries and solar cells, are growing rapidly. Chinese brands will account for 67 percent of new energy vehicle sales in ASEAN in 2023. The scale of cooperation in clean energy such as wind power, hydropower and solar energy continued to expand. Second, blue economy cooperation has been strengthened. In September 2023, the China - ASEAN Leaders ' Meeting proposed to maximize the role of the blue economy in achieving economic growth, improving social inclusiveness, improving people 's living standards and

---

[1] Rencheng District Commerce Bureau. New opportunities for China–Singapore economic and trade cooperation [EB/OL]. (2024 – 01 – 01) [2024 – 07 – 31]. http://www. rencheng.gov.cn/ art/2024/1/1/art_73208_2780460.html.

protecting the environment. In 2023, China's Marine economy will account for 7.9% of GDP, with large room for improvement. More than 94% of China's foreign trade is carried out by sea, while 60% of ASEAN's foreign trade is carried out by sea. 65% of trade between China and ASEAN is carried out by sea. In addition, China and ASEAN have strong complementarity and great potential for cooperation in digital economy, and digital economic cooperation will become a new driving force for the growth of China - ASEAN bilateral trade.[1] Cross - border e - commerce, as a new form and model of trade, has become an important factor to enhance China-ASEAN economic and trade ties and effectively mitigate the impact of the epidemic on trade. Chinese e-commerce platforms are accelerating the pace of building overseas warehouses in Southeast Asian countries. Under the background of RCEP coming into effect and the normalization of online economy, as well as government support and market efforts, cross-border e-commerce cooperation between China and ASEAN has broad prospects.[2]

2.1.4　New progress in China-ASEAN institutional opening-up

The two sides have made steady progress in institutional opening - up and cooperation on rules, regulations, management and standards in the region. Negotiations on the 3.0 version of the CAFTA have been accelerated. The Standardization Cooperation and Exchange Center of ASEAN countries has been launched in Nanning. China and ASEAN will seize the opportunity of digital economy development to build digital economy and governance rules

---

① ［EB/OL］. （2024-05-25）［2024-07-31］. http://www.people.com.cn/.
② ［EB/OL］. （2022-09-25）［2024-07-31］. http://www.people.com.cn/.

applicable to developing countries. First, we will make use of existing digital economy agreements. RCEP, CPTPP and DEPA all cover digital trade rules. We can choose to join any agreement according to their respective digital economy development process and governance concept to enhance the flexibility of joining the agreement. By participating in these agreements to promote the development of our own digital economy, participate in improving the content of these agreements, and guide future digital cooperation. In this way, it is conducive to promoting the establishment of fairer and more balanced international digital economic relations, helping countries to grasp the initiative and discourse of digital governance, and avoiding being marginalized by developed countries in the global digital economic system, or being forced to accept a highly liberalized digital economic system. The second is to use existing digital cooperation methods. Strengthen digital economy cooperation between China and ASEAN countries through the "Digital Silk Road", and share their respective technologies and experiences in areas such as digital infrastructure construction, e-commerce development and smart city construction.

2.2　Key points of China–ASEAN economic and trade cooperation

2.2.1　Deepen and strengthen connectivity

The China-Laos railway has enjoyed strong passenger and cargo growth, the China-Laos Thai-Malaysia cross-border railway train has been officially put into operation, and the new Western Land-Sea Corridor rail-sea combined transport train has deepened the integration of production and supply chains of all parties, thus deepening China - ASEAN connectivity. The Jakarta - Bandung high-speed Railway is the first high-speed railway in Indonesia and Southeast Asia and a flagship project of practical cooperation between China and Indonesia. The operation of the Jakarta - Bandung high - speed Railway has not only improved local traffic conditions and made it more convenient for people to travel along the route, but also boosted business development and tourism, injecting new impetus into regional economic and social development. It is an important symbol of cooperation between China and Indonesia. In addition, during the construction of the Jakarta-Bandung high-speed railway, a total of 51,000 local people have been hired and 45,000 Indonesian employees have been trained.[1]

2.2.2　Integration of the digital economy

China and ASEAN continue to improve their economic and trade cooperation mechanisms. The China - ASEAN Expo, the China - ASEAN Business and Investment Summit, the China - ASEAN Information Port and other important economic and trade platforms have greatly promoted the docking and implementation of China-ASEAN projects in digital-related fields. The ASEAN market has attracted a large number of leading enterprises in China 's digital realm, including e - commerce platforms such as Alibaba, Tencent and Jingdong, mobile payment enterprises such as Ant Group, and digital enterprises such as Huawei and ZTE. These Chinese enterprises have deeply

---

[1]　Sun Lei, Xinhua News Agency: The Jakarta-Bandung high-speed railway has been officially put into operation[EB/OL]. (2023-10-18) [2024-07-31]. http://www.xinhua-net.com/2023-10/18/c_1129923113.htm

cooperated with ASEAN digital enterprises such as Tokopedia and Lazada to promote advanced Internet technologies and mature business models, and drive the development of related industries and the construction of digital connectivity in ASEAN.[①]

2.2.3　Green, low-carbon and high-quality development

China and ASEAN are natural partners in green economy with strong complementarity in natural resources, production capacity and industrial structure. The Chinese government will implement the concept of green development, actively develop ecological and environmental protection, sustainable energy and other industries, build a green, low-carbon and circular economic system, and lay a solid foundation for China - ASEAN cooperation on green economy and investment. In recent years, the two sides have vigorously promoted policy dialogue, exchanges and cooperation in such areas as circular economy, energy conservation and environmental protection, green energy, sustainable finance and climate change.

China and ASEAN have significant complementary advantages in the field of new energy vehicles and broad prospects for cooperation. At the industrial level, ASEAN leaders have reached consensus on the development of a regional electric vehicle ecosystem, and member states have introduced investment incentive policies for relevant industries. Some member states are rich in nickel, rare earth and other resources, which provides a good

---

① Sun Lei, Xinhua News Agency: The Jakarta–Bandung high-speed railway has been officially put into operation[EB/OL]. (2023-10-18) [2024-07-31]. http://www.xinhua-net.com/2023-10-18/c_1129923113.htm

foundation for industrial and supply chain cooperation. At the consumption level, Singapore has released a blueprint for green transportation development. Thailand plans to achieve 50% of new car registration of pure electric vehicles by 2030. The Philippines requires domestic public transport enterprises to increase the proportion of pure electric vehicles to more than 5% .Indonesia will introduce subsidies for electric car purchases from 2023, it plans to increase the share of electric vehicle sales to 25% by 2025.[1]

2.3   Difficulties in China–ASEAN economic and trade cooperation

2.3.1   Imbalances in trade in goods remain

China's trade balances with Singapore and Vietnam in 2023 both exceeded ＄45 billion, while its deficit with Malaysia exceeded ＄15 billion. China attaches great importance to the issue of trade imbalance with ASEAN, actively adopts a variety of wording to properly solve it, promote the sound development of bilateral trade, and consolidate the strategic partnership with ASEAN under the new development pattern.

Continue to promote trade liberalization and facilitation and expand imports from ASEAN member states. First, continue to unilaterally expand the scope of zero - tariff products to Cambodia, Laos, Myanmar and other ASEAN members. Second, high - quality implementation of free trade agreements such as the Regional Comprehensive Economic Partnership (RCEP). Make full use of the rules and regulations of free trade agreements, especially the

---

① Southeast Asia is tapping China for electric cars[EB/OL].(2023－12－12)[2024－07－31]. https://www.163.com/dy/article/ ILPH1FVM0514BQ68.html.

RCEP, cumulative rules of Origin, and tariff reduction for more than 90% of products, to further expand imports from ASEAN members. Third, continue to give full play to the role of exhibition platforms such as the Import Expo, the ASEAN Expo and the Xiamen Investment Fair. Strengthening exchanges, cooperation and consultation with ASEAN member states can enrich the contents of these exhibition platforms, set up or continue to set up special exhibition platforms for products of ASEAN member states, publicize their products and services, and give full play to the advantages of China's super-large domestic market, which is conducive to expanding the export of products of ASEAN member states to China. In addition, continue to promote trade liberalization and facilitation, strengthen customs cooperation with ASEAN member states and mutual recognition of qualifications to facilitate customs clearance and efficient operation.

Second, continue to advocate investment liberalization and facilitation and increase the scale of China's investment in ASEAN. Taking into account East Asian culture, regional advantages and rules of industrial transfer, China has taken the lead in transferring industries to ASEAN member states and increasing investment in ASEAN. Give full play to the linkage effect of investment and trade, further increase imports from ASEAN member states, and form a win-win development pattern for all. Make full use of bilateral and multilateral agreements to help enterprises invest effectively. In addition, continue to foster a favorable environment for peaceful development, strengthen cooperation with more than 200 sister cities in ASEAN, and carry out project cooperation in areas such as disaster management, narrowing the development gap, and connectivity construction, so as to release the dividends of our country's economic and social development, especially to accelerate the economic recovery process of ASEAN member states under the new situation after the pandemic.

Third, standardize advanced international rules and build high - quality overseas economic and trade cooperation zones. First, strengthen cooperation with ASEAN and its member states, implement the RCEP with high quality, jointly build a free trade area with the largest population, the largest economic and trade scale and the greatest development potential in the world, promote trade and investment liberalization and facilitation, and further unleash huge effects. Second, to comply with high-level international advanced rules such as green development and environmental protection, actively build pilot free trade zones, Hainan Free Trade Ports and overseas economic and trade cooperation zones, and strengthen the cooperation among these special economic zones, which will help Chinese enterprises master international rules, adapt to the regulatory requirements of ASEAN member states and improve their international competitiveness. Third, further optimize the layout and development plan of overseas economic and trade cooperation zones, improve their operation quality, give full play to the complementary advantages of goods trade, service trade and investment cooperation with ASEAN member states, explore the international division of labor cooperation mode with deep integration of industrial chain, supply chain and value chain, consolidate the foundation of "Belt and Road" cooperation, and further improve the level and quality of cooperation between China and ASEAN member states.[1]

2.3.2　Industrial and supply chain cooperations face challenges

The backflow of manufacturing industries in developed countries makes it more difficult for China-ASEAN manufacturing industries to improve their "chain position" in the global industrial chain. ASEAN has become an important player in safeguarding regional industrial and supply chain security. At present, China and ASEAN have formed a mutually beneficial "regional circulation" model in which ASEAN exports primary goods to China, imports machinery and equipment (capital intensive) and intermediate goods (technology intensive) from China, and then exports consumer goods (labor intensive) to China and a third country. In addition, ASEAN has obvious comparative advantages in energy, minerals, agriculture and other fields, so it is urgent to enhance and optimize the China-ASEAN industrial chain and supply chain. The two sides need to open up and jointly build a more resilient China-ASEAN industrial chain and supply chain, focus on stabilizing China-ASEAN industrial chain and supply chain, and pragmatically advance the process of active opening-up to ASEAN. This process aims to achieve a major breakthrough in China-ASEAN free trade, focuses on improving the integration and sustainability of industrial and supply chains, relies on the existing regional and sub-regional cooperation mechanisms and infrastructure networks, and takes country-by-country and step-by-step

---

①　China Economic Times. Multi-ways to solve the problem of trade imbalance with ASEAN[EB/OL].(2023-05-15)[2024-07-31] http://fta.mofcom.gov. cn/ article/china-dongmengupgrade/chinadongmengupgradegfguandian/202305/539251.html.

progress as the basic strategy. For example, taking the lead in the field of trade in goods and expanding to trade in services; take the lead in the land domain, and expand to the Marine domain; take the lead in implementing it in the economic and trade field and expand it to the social field.

2.3.3　Cooperation in the digital economy requires further enhancement

At present, the main rules of digital economic cooperation between China and ASEAN still have shortcomings in the specific implementation process. First, the integrity of the content is insufficient. The content of digital economy focuses on the chapter of e - commerce, which only includes the basic provisions of the development of digital economy, but does not involve digital products, digital technology and source code and other important emerging issues of digital economy. Second, the content accuracy is not enough. RCEP not only emphasizes cross-border data transmission, but also attaches importance to the balance between free data flow and national sovereignty and security. However, the specific implementation details of cross-border data transmission are still in a vague state. Therefore, it still faces many risks and problems in the actual operation process. Third, it is difficult to unify regional cooperation. As the largest free trade agreement, RCEP has different digital economy development concepts and development processes among the 10 member states of ASEAN. It is a major level to unify the regional internal digital economy cooperation concepts and development measures.

The digital economic cooperation between China and ASEAN should be guided by the existing digital economic and trade rules, improve the cooperation mode and deepen the cooperation content, and promote the negotiation and signing of the "China - ASEAN Digital Economic Cooperation Agreement", so as to improve the accuracy of cooperation. China and ASEAN should seize the opportunity of digital economy development, create digital trade and governance rules applicable to developing countries, break through the unfair monopoly and oppression of hegemons, create a fair and sustainable environment for digital development, make their own voices heard, and benefit developing countries around the world while finding a digital development path that belongs to developing countries. As the initiator of the Belt and Road Initiative, China can strengthen digital economy cooperation with the co-building countries through the Digital Silk Road, and share its technology and experience in the fields of digital infrastructure construction, e-commerce development and smart city construction.

2.3.4 Improvement of economic and trade quality and efficiency must overcome institutional barriers

In bilateral economic and trade cooperation, there are still problems such as logistics blockage at unimpeded ports, inconvenient cross - border RMB settlement, and inconsistent transport standards and rules. First of all, as the dividends of RCEP policies continue to be released, the scale of China's cross-border e - commerce transactions with ASEAN continues to expand, and it is urgent to break through the blockage points of multimodal transport and improve the efficiency of goods flow. Business innovation will be carried out in the customs transfer link to realize the "non-sensitive" customs transfer mode, paperless operation of the whole customs transfer, automatic unlocking of electronic lock, automatic verification of customs transfer data, etc., which will greatly improve the timeliness of goods transportation. To address market pain points, we will promote trade facilitation reform, foster and develop new forms of trade, and accelerate the formation of ASEAN-oriented cross-border e-commerce industrial clusters. Secondly, the clearing mode has drawbacks, and the efficiency of cross-border clearing needs to be improved. Insufficient sources of offshore RMB and lack of overseas investment channels limit the market development scale of cross-border RMB business.[①]In addition, institutional innovation is the core task for the unification of transport standards and rules in bilateral economic and trade cooperation. China (Guangxi) Pilot Free Trade Zone (Guangxi Pilot Free Trade Zone for short) focuses on the three major characteristics of ASEAN, serving the new land-sea corridor in western China, and opening up along the border. It has actively carried out differentiated exploration and institutional innovation with its own characteristics, and has explored and formulated five batches of 169 institutional innovation achievements at the autonomous region level.[②]

---

① Risk prevention of cross-border RMB business between China and ASEAN[EB/OL].(2019.12.23)[2024.07.31]. http://shop. chinaforex. com.cn/magazine/pages/dgarticle.vc? article=48608.

② Guangxi Daily official website, Zhou Hongmei: Guangxi Pilot Free Trade Zone reform test field harvest new "abundant" scene[EB/OL].(2024-5-29)[2024-07-31]. http://www.gxrb.com.cn.

III Prospects of China−ASEAN economic and trade cooperation in 2025

3.1 Trade in goods

3.1.1 Continue to expand China−ASEAN trade cooperation

The economies of China and ASEAN countries are obviously complementary, which has laid a solid foundation for bilateral trade cooperation. The two sides have broad consistency in industrial chain, supply chain and market demand. At the same time, the two sides share common interests in green economy, digital economy and other emerging fields, attach great importance to economic transformation and upgrading, and actively seek new economic growth points. Economic and trade cooperation enjoys strong momentum and broad space.

The in-depth implementation of the RCEP policy and the rapid progress of the China-ASEAN Free Trade Area version 3.0 have created more promising trade expectations and created favorable conditions for unleashing the trade potential of the two sides. On the one hand, with the in-depth implementation of RCEP and other policies, according to the trade diversion effect, the supply chain network between China and ASEAN economies will be more resilient and the trade relations between the two sides will be more stable; On the other hand, the two sides will actively promote the construction of free trade zones, break down various barriers to trade cooperation, give full play to the effect of super-large market scale, further expand the breadth and depth of trade cooperation, and open up broader space for cooperation.

China is accelerating the building of a unified national market, deepening market-oriented reform of factors of production, and aligning itself with high-standard international economic and trade rules, thus injecting new vitality into China-ASEAN economic and trade cooperation. ASEAN countries have also actively promoted the reform of their domestic economic systems, stepped up economic opening, created a favorable domestic market environment for foreign trade and economic cooperation, and effectively promoted the deepening of China-ASEAN trade cooperation.

3.1.2   Deepen China—ASEAN green trade cooperation represented by the " New Three" products

ASEAN countries have actively promoted the development of the new energy vehicle (NEV) industry. Malaysia plans to build about 10, 000 public charging facilities across the country by 2025, with electric vehicles accounting for 15% of the country's total car sales by 2030. The Thai government has lowered import tariffs on new energy vehicles and parts, and provided vehicle purchase subsidies for buyers. Indonesia has set a goal of becoming an electric vehicle manufacturing and export hub in Southeast Asia, aiming to increase production to one million electric vehicles by 2035. These measures provide a broad market space and strong policy support for

China and ASEAN to carry out green trade cooperation.

In the field of photovoltaic, the Vietnamese government approved the release of the Eighth Electricity Development Plan (PDP VIII) on April 1, 2024, which aims to significantly expand the scale of photovoltaic power plants and energy storage capacity by 2030. The Philippine government has included green ecosystem industries such as renewable energy and energy storage as "priority industries for foreign investment" and given tax incentives of different degrees and durations. The realization of the goal of energy transformation requires the support of capital, technology and infrastructure. However, China's photovoltaic module output has ranked first in the world for 16 consecutive years, and the output and capacity of polysilicon, silicon wafer, cell wafer and module account for more than 80% of the world, with obvious technological and cost advantages. This has laid a foundation for cooperation between China and ASEAN in the field of new energy. The two sides have complementary advantages and great potential for cooperation.

In the field of new energy batteries, data released by the China Association of Automobile Manufacturers show that China has applied for 74% of the world's power battery patents, and has become one of the world's major technology sources in the field of lithium batteries and solid-state batteries. Chinese companies such as BYD and CATL have obvious technological advantages in developing new energy batteries. Thanks to the accumulation and upgrading effect of technology, China's international technological competitiveness in green economic fields such as new energy will be further strengthened in the future, which lays a solid foundation for deepening green trade cooperation between China and ASEAN countries and provides a strong technological driving force.

3.1.3　Actively promote China-ASEAN digital trade cooperation

China will give full play to its advantages in digital technology and digital infrastructure to provide accurate information and technical assistance to backward regions in ASEAN countries that lack digital conditions. Through customized solutions, not only the hardware facilities in these areas will be improved, but also the innovation of information mode will be promoted, and a digital infrastructure system integrating multiple technologies and highly compatible systems will be built. This will fundamentally solve the problems of low connectivity and serious information islands in current cooperation, and promote the sustainable development of China - ASEAN digital trade cooperation.

China and ASEAN will continue to build a complete and efficient digital trade ecosystem, including cross-border e-commerce platform, supply chain management platform, logistics platform and enterprise sales APP, to provide solid platform support for digital trade cooperation between the two sides. At the same time, the two sides should vigorously build digital cross-border logistics channels, build digital trade logistics service centers, and promote the digitalization of the whole process of customs clearance and transportation. For example, in the future, the two sides can cooperate to explore the construction of an efficient digital logistics information collaborative platform, and use cloud computing, Internet of Things, big data and other technologies to connect with domestic and foreign logistics enterprise systems, comprehensive foreign trade service platforms and customs information service platforms, so as to provide all-subject, all-link and all-weather logistics information services in real time and effectively improve cross-border logistics efficiency. We will accelerate high-level connectivity. In the future, China and ASEAN should actively participate in the negotiation of global digital trade rules and enhance their discourse power in digital trade rules of both sides. At the same time, when China and ASEAN carry out digital trade cooperation, it should actively share its own experience in digital trade governance, so as to help ASEAN countries improve their digital trade system, constantly optimize the framework of China-ASEAN digital trade cooperation, and promote the sustainable and in-depth development of China-ASEAN digital trade cooperation.

3.2　Two-way investment

3.2.1　Global industrial chain and supply chain adjustments create new investment opportunities

At present, the adjustment of the global industrial chain and supply chain is accelerating, and ASEAN has become an important subject to maintain the security of the regional industrial chain and supply chain. China and ASEAN have gradually formed a "regional circulation" model of mutualbenefit and win-win results in the industrial chain and supply chain. In 2023, China's trade with ASEAN will account for 15.3 percent of China's total trade. Among them, the import and export of intermediate goods accounted for 64.4% of the total bilateral import and export. The comparative advantages of ASEAN countries in energy, minerals, agriculture and other sectors as well as the diversity of their economies provide a wide range of options for Chinese partners seeking to diversify their supply chains. It is expected that in 2025, the industries in which China and ASEAN have comparative advantages in the industrial chain and supply chain will become the hot spots of bilateral investment.

3.2.2   Full implementation of RCEP unleashes demand for investment in the service sector

In 2023, the Regional Comprehensive Economic Partnership Agreement (RCEP) will come into full force in ASEAN countries. According to the agreement, member states will gradually open more than 65% of their service sectors within 15 years, including finance, communication, education, medical care, tourism, culture and other fields. This will create huge opportunities for two-way investment between China and ASEAN in the service sector. It is expected that in 2025, with the in-depth implementation of RCEP, two-way investment between China and ASEAN in the service sector will be further expanded and deepened. Cooperation between the two sides in finance, education, medical care, tourism, culture and ICT will inject new impetus into regional economic growth and social development.

3.2.3   Huge investment potential in the infrastructure sector

At present, ASEAN countries are actively promoting infrastructure modernization, and there is huge potential in infrastructure construction. According to the forecast of the International Monetary Fund (IMF), the infrastructure investment demand of ASEAN countries will reach about 2.1

trillion US dollars by 2024, which provides a huge market space for China-ASEAN bilateral cooperation. At the same time, China has rich experience and technological advantages in infrastructure construction, and has world-leading competitiveness in high-speed rail, ports, energy grids and other infrastructure sectors, which fully meets ASEAN's demand for infrastructure modernization. It is expected that in 2025, the investment of China and ASEAN in the field of infrastructure will be further deepened, and the advantages of Chinese enterprises in capital, technology and management will be combined with the market and resource advantages of ASEAN countries, so as to widely participate in the infrastructure construction projects of ASEAN countries and jointly promote the upgrading and improvement of regional infrastructure. We will further promote connectivity and regional integration.

3.2.4　Burgeoning cooperation in the digital economy

By 2025, the digital economy of ASEAN countries will be worth about $ 1 trillion, or more than 20 percent of regional GDP, according to McKinsey. At the same time, China has the world's largest population of Internet users and highly developed digital infrastructure, with significant advantages in areas such as e-commerce, mobile payment, artificial intelligence and big data. In 2023, the scale of China's digital economy will exceed 55 trillion yuan, and the value added of core industries in the digital economy will account for about 10% of GDP. This fully demonstrates the huge potential and broad prospects of China-ASEAN cooperation in the digital economy. In 2022, China and ASEAN signed the Action Plan for the Implementation of the China - ASEAN Digital Economy Partnership (2021—2025) to continuously strengthen cooperation in the field of digital economy. It is expected that in 2024, digital economy will continue to be an important area of two - way investment between China and ASEAN. The two sides will further strengthen cooperation in e-commerce, fintech, digital infrastructure, smart cities and other aspects to promote bilateral investment in digital economy and realize the beautiful vision of promoting common development through digital economy.

3.2.5 Broad prospects for investment in green and low-carbon economy

The Southeast Asia Green Economy Report 2022 estimates that ASEAN countries need to invest between US $ 1 trillion and US $ 3 trillion to meet their 2030 carbon reduction targets, and that energy demand in ASEAN countries will increase by nearly 50 percent by 2030. At the same time, China has rich experience and technological advantages in green and low-carbon economy, and is also a world leader in technology and industrialization capabilities in solar, wind and nuclear energy. By 2023, China's installed renewable energy capacity will reach 1.2 billion kilowatts, accounting for more than 30% of the world's total. In addition, Chinese enterprises have helped ASEAN countries improve energy efficiency and achieve energy conservation and emission reduction. In 2022, they jointly established the "China-Singapore Green Finance Cooperation Demonstration Zone" with Singapore to further promote cooperation in green finance. It is expected that in 2025, China- ASEAN cooperation in renewable energy, energy conservation and emission reduction, green finance and other aspects will be further deepened, laying a solid foundation for sustainable development of regional economy and making important contributions to the realization of global climate goals.

3.3   Trade in services

Under the superimposed opportunities of RCEP and China-ASEAN version 3.0 negotiations, the main obstacles to China-ASEAN free trade have shifted from tariff barriers in the field of goods trade to regulation, non - tariff barriers and market openness in the field of service trade and investment. China and ASEAN should further strengthen cooperation in key areas, deepen two-way investment, and promote the free flow of service elements, so as to promote the further development of service trade.

3.3.1   Deepen reform and opening up in key areas of the service sector

Consolidate the development of traditional service sectors such as tourism, transportation, and other business services. Tourism service is an important part of the service trade between China and ASEAN. Although COVID- 19 has had a great impact on tourism, ASEAN countries have advantages in tourism service export, such as rich tourism resources, relatively complete supporting facilities, and relatively complete upstream and downstream industries. At the same time, China's tourism resources are heterogeneous, and it has similar cultural background to ASEAN countries, so the two sides have a large space for cooperation in tourism cooperation. Transport services are increasingly in demand. With the adjustment of industrial structure in China and developed countries, more and more industries have been transferred to Vietnam, Thailand, Indonesia and other regions. The construction of China-ASEAN regional industrial chain will drive the development of transportation, finance and other related services. As a traditional service sector in China-ASEAN cooperation, transportation services will stimulate new growth points and growth potential. The trading scale of bulk products represented by palm oil, iron ore, natural gas and rice continues to rise, which will not only drive the construction of bulk commodity logistics systems between China and ASEAN, but also usher in new development in the transportation industry.

Accelerate industrial cooperation in emerging service sectors such as finance and insurance, telecommunications, computers and other emerging service areas. Finance and insurance, telecommunications and computers are the key areas of China-ASEAN cooperation. Bilateral trade is growing rapidly, but it is still small. With the construction of RCEP and China-ASEAN Version 3.0, China-ASEAN financial insurance, telecommunications, computers, etc., will face lower market access threshold, and service trade barriers will be further reduced. Under the background of continuous improvement of regional industrial chain and adjustment of industrial layout, finance and insurance, telecommunications and computers will become the growth poles of regional service trade development. Sensitive sectors such as telecommunications, finance and insurance should be further opened up, market-based development of finance and telecommunications should be supported, and transnational cooperative development should be encouraged.

3.3.2　Explore the construction of a high – standard new digital economy environment

First of all, a platform for cross-border exchange and information sharing should be built to promote cross-border trade cooperation in the region. Based on the characteristics of China and ASEAN countries, we should cooperate with relevant departments, research institutions or universities of countries in the region to establish a multi-language database of supply and demand information of service enterprises, and share the information of investment environment, trade policy, talent exchange, project supply and demand, financing solutions and other information of each country by category. Second, establish and improve the data sharing mechanism. Build a data sharing platform between governments, expand the scope of data sharing, release a shared data catalog, build a data sharing platform and governance mechanism, and promote the establishment of international rules for the digital economy. Standardize cross-border data flow, build a high-standard data security management certification system, build new rules for safe, high-standard and convenient cross-border data flow, and form basic rules for regional cross-border data flow.

3.3.3　Impove regulatory environment to promote the integration of trade and investment

The governments of China and ASEAN should vigorously develop the service industry, optimize the business environment, and provide material conditions for expanding the export of service trade. On the one hand, while

ASEAN countries such as Thailand, Vietnam and Indonesia continue to strengthen infrastructure construction, the governments should introduce relevant supportive policies to attract more investment to ASEAN, and guide more investment inside and outside the region to flow into emerging service industries such as computer, financial services, insurance and accounting, and scientific and technological services, so as to cultivate knowledge-intensive service trade enterprises and form industrial clusters. On the other hand, China should continue to release positive policy signals, remove the regulation of competition as much as possible, reduce policy uncertainty, simplify administrative examination and approval procedures, reduce transaction costs, improve enterprise transaction efficiency, strengthen market expectations, and promote the integrated development of trade and investment.

3.3.4　Promote the cross-regional mobility of natural persons

Personnel training and technological progress are the source and power of the development of trade in services, so we should actively promote the training of talents in trade in services and the cross-regional flow of personnel elements. First of all, under the framework of RCEP, China and ASEAN should further lower the flow threshold of professional and technical talents, gradually improve the flow mechanism of natural persons, and encourage the flow of talents. Build a platform mechanism for the cross-border flow of talents between China and ASEAN, smooth the exchange of talents between the two sides, promote the cross-border flow of talents, and then introduce advanced technology and management experience, and promote the exchange of experience, technology and management experience. In terms of talent training, we should promote international educational exchanges and cooperation, promote China-ASEAN university cooperation, promote cross-regional exchanges of high-quality talents, and cultivate international talents. In addition, it is necessary to simplify the entry and exit travel procedures between China and ASEAN, give full play to the role of policies such as transit visa-free, stimulate two-way tourism between China and ASEAN countries, improve the convenience of tourism, strengthen cultural exchanges between China and ASEAN, and promote the cultural communication and influence of both sides.

3.4 Prospects of business opportunities of CAFTA 3.0

3.4.1 The opportunities of CAFTA 3.0 for enterprises

First, market scope expands and access opportunities increase. The CAFTA is one of the free trade areas with the largest population coverage and the fastest growth rate in the world, with a huge consumer market of 1.9 billion people, enterprises can more easily enter these markets, absorb new consumer groups, and expand their market share. In addition, with the improvement of trade facilitation, the barriers for enterprise products to enter the markets of countries in the region are further reduced, which accelerates the free circulation of goods in the region. In addition, the upgrade of the free trade zone also creates more opportunities in terms of investment, laying a foundation for the long-term development of enterprises.

Second, reduce enterprise costs and improve enterprise benefits. In terms of product production, by reducing tariff and non-tariff barriers among member countries, the import prices of raw materials and intermediate products have been reduced, and the production costs of products have been reduced. In addition, with the deepening of supply chain connectivity in the region, the efficiency of cooperation between enterprises and upstream and downstream industries has been continuously improved, and resources have been used more efficiently. In terms of logistics and transportation costs, infrastructure construction improves the connectivity and operational efficiency of logistics networks and reduces the total transportation costs. At the same time, with the improvement of the level of trade facilitation, the transparency and consistency of the system, the compliance cost of enterprises is further compressed.

Third, strengthen technological cooperation and increase innovation opportunities. Accelerating alignment with international economic and trade rules, deepening technological and economic cooperation, and promoting technological innovation and industrial upgrading of enterprises. In terms of technology upgrading, we will guide enterprises to strengthen investment in research and development and support the application of new technologies, processes and materials. At the same time, we will accelerate the upgrading of traditional industries, focus on digitalization and sustainable development, and promote the formation of a more efficient industrial growth model. In addition, enterprises can actively expand international cooperation opportunities with the help of the free trade zone platform. In terms of IPR protection, we will strengthen the revision of relevant laws and regulations, carry out international legal cooperation, establish a more efficient IPR protection system, and stimulate innovation vitality.

Fourth, we should grasp new growth points and realize modern development. Digital economy and green economy represent the trend of future economic development, and the upgrading of the free trade zone provides new growth points and opportunities for the development of enterprises in these fields. First of all, the digital economy and green economy themselves have a huge market space, and consumers' demand for digital and sustainable products and services will continue to grow. Secondly, enterprises can also combine the original business with digital and green, improve the decision-making level and the efficiency of enterprise operations through digital integration, assume social responsibility through sustainable development, and improve the social image of enterprises.

3.4.2 The opportunities of CAFTA 3.0 for China

First, grasp the two markets and two resources to promote the construction of a double cycle pattern. The construction of the CAFTA version 3.0 not only means that Chinese enterprises can more easily enter the ASEAN market, but also provides a broader space for the products and services of ASEAN countries to enter the Chinese market. Through such a two-way open market, China can make better use of both domestic and international resources and markets, promote the construction of a new development pattern, and build an economic pattern in which the major domestic cycle is the main body and the double domestic and international cycles reinforce each other. By deepening economic cooperation with ASEAN countries,

China will also respond more effectively to changes in the external economic environment and enhance the resilience and resilience of its economy.

Second, accelerate the replacement of old drivers of growth with new ones and upgrading the economic structure. With the rapid development of China's economy, the traditional economic growth model is difficult to adapt to the development of the times. Therefore, it is necessary to accelerate the transformation of traditional industries to the direction of high - end, intelligent and green, cultivate and strengthen emerging industries, and form new economic growth points. Emerging industries can achieve rapid development by virtue of more preferential policies and development opportunities in the free trade zone, and contribute to the optimization and upgrading of China's economic structure. With the mutual opening of markets, new consumer demands are created, prompting Chinese enterprises to develop new products and services that meet market demands, and promoting consumption upgrading and industrial restructuring.

Third, enhance political mutual trust and promote regional stability. The CAFTA plays an important role in enhancing political mutual trust and promoting regional stability. The FTA provides a platform for multilateral exchanges and cooperation among member states, and regular consultation and dialogue mechanisms have enhanced mutual trust and understanding. In addition, the increase in the number of projects and personnel exchanges in the CAFTA has enhanced the friendship between the two peoples and laid a social foundation for political mutual trust.

3.4.3 The opportunities of CAFTA 3.0 for ASEAN

First, we need to accelerate economic development and improve social well-being. First of all, the FTA has further opened the Chinese market for the featured products of ASEAN countries, which has brought significant export growth and foreign exchange earnings to ASEAN countries. Secondly, under the FTA framework, ASEAN countries actively attract international investment and accelerate the transformation and upgrading of economic structure. On this basis, a large number of employment opportunities have been generated, and with the increase in employment rate and income, the scale of the poor population has further decreased, and the overall level of social well-being has been significantly improved.

Second, accelerate infrastructure development to achieve connectivity. The free trade area can bring more financial support and rich experience to ASEAN countries, and accelerate regional connectivity through infrastructure construction. A more efficient transportation and logistics network will promote the free flow of resources in the region, effectively reduce transaction costs, provide a more flexible and resilient supply chain for enterprises in the region, and the overall operational efficiency is expected to be further improved. In addition, increased connectivity not only improves economic efficiency, but also enhances citizens' access to more equitable social resources through more reliable transportation facilities and more efficient communication networks.

Third, speed up the transfer of skills and knowledge. The construction of the CAFTA version 3.0 not only brings economic benefits to ASEAN countries, but also promotes the effective transfer of skills and knowledge. Under the

FTA framework, ASEAN countries can more easily import advanced production technology and experience from China. In terms of educational cooperation, ASEAN countries have actively enhanced exchanges and cooperation with Chinese institutions to improve the learning opportunities of ASEAN students in China. Through these measures, ASEAN countries can also adapt and adjust to local conditions according to their actual conditions to achieve more effective social development and economic growth.

3.4.4   The economic and trade potential of CAFTA 3.0

First, ASEAN's economic performance has continued to improve. As shown in Figure 8, since 2013, ASEAN's GDP has always shown a steady growth trend, from 2.51 trillion US dollars to 3.62 trillion US dollars in 2022. This growth demonstrates ASEAN's competitiveness in the global economy and the attractiveness of ASEAN markets to outside investors. Especially in 2017 and 2022, the GDP growth rate reached 5.4% and 5.6% respectively, showing strong economic growth momentum. ASEAN economies have also demonstrated strong resilience. In particular, after experiencing a short-term economic recession in 2020, it recovered rapidly in the following year, and the total GDP exceeded the level of the year before the decline, which shows that ASEAN countries have the ability to take effective policy measures to cope with the challenges of economic uncertainty.

Second, ASEAN's population has grown steadily and incomes have continued to rise. As shown in Figure 9, from 2013 to 2022, ASEAN's population grew from 612 million to 671 million, with an annual growth rate of about 1%, and the labor market and consumer market expanded year by year. The growth of population provides a broader market space for Chinese enterprises, especially in the fields of basic living needs and services. ASEAN's per capita GDP grew from US $ 4, 105. 20 in 2013 to US $ 5, 391.80 in 2022, as residents' income levels rise and consumption up-grades, increasing consumer demand for high-quality goods and services. The two factors interact and jointly promote the economic and trade cooperation and regional economic integration process between China and ASEAN.

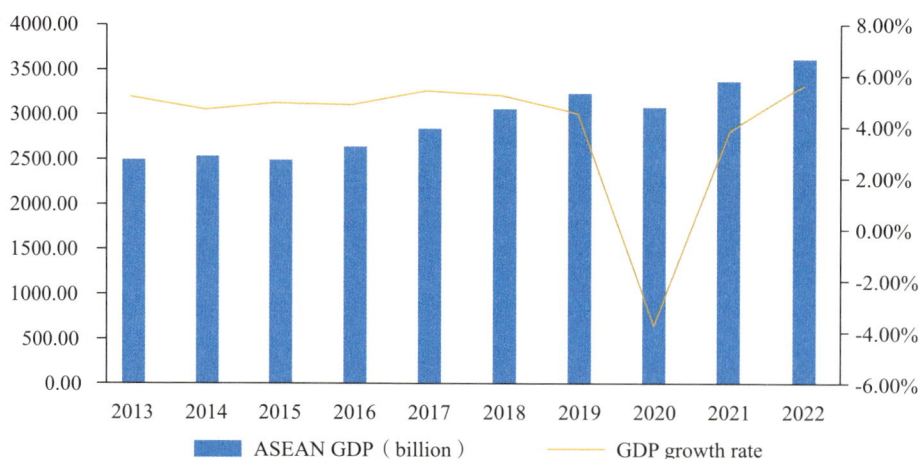

Figure 8   Total GDP and its growth rate of ASEAN

Source: ASEAN Statistical Yearbook

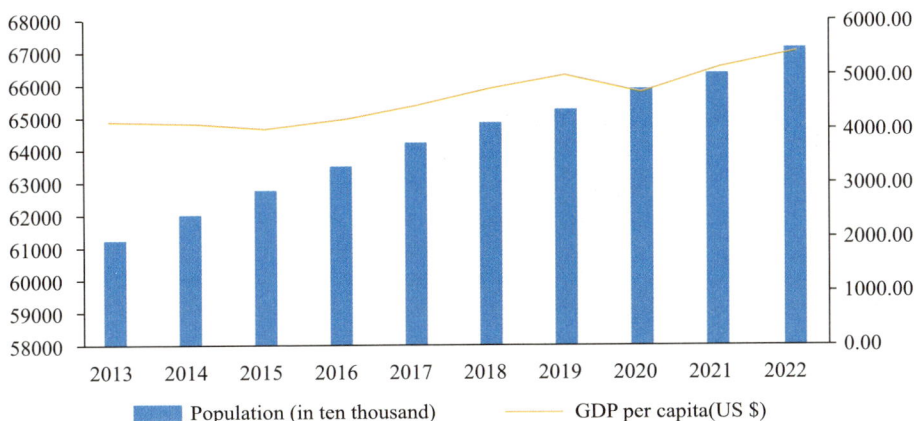

Figure 9　Total population and GDP per capita in ASEAN

Source: ASEAN Statistical Yearbook

Third, the industrial structure has been constantly improved. As shown in Figure 10, the manufacturing sector has the highest share of 21.20% in the ASEAN economy. With the upgrading of China's manufacturing industry, some labor - intensive and resource - intensive industries are moving to ASEAN, which not only brings job opportunities and technology transfer to ASEAN, but also provides new investment hotspots and market space for Chinese entrepreneurs. Finance and insurance, information and communication, public administration and other service activities are also important components of the ASEAN economy, accounting for 6.70 percent, 4 percent, and 10. 30 percent, respectively. These areas provide opportunities for cooperation, especially in fintech, digital construction and infrastructure investment.

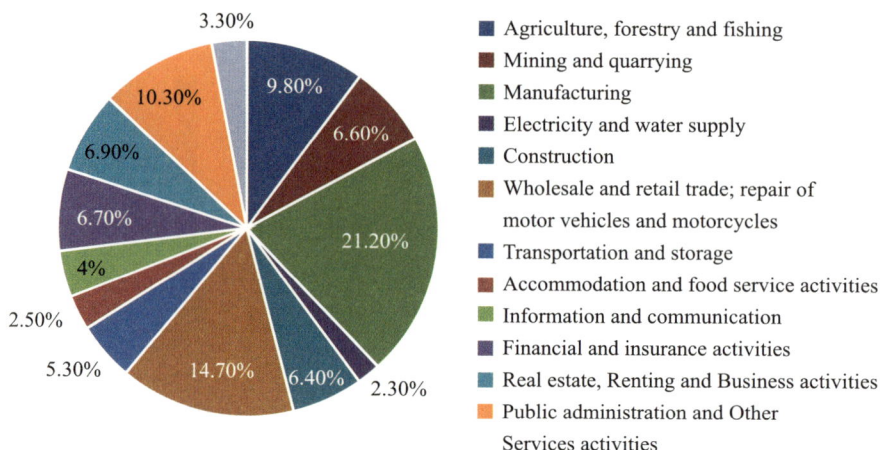

Figure 10   Share of ASEAN industries in 2022

Source: ASEAN Statistical Yearbook

Fourth, the level of China - ASEAN trade is relatively high. Since the establishment of the CAFTA, bilateral economic and trade exchanges have grown rapidly. With the RCEP coming into force and the construction of a new land - sea corridor in western China, the scale of bilateral trade has further expanded. From 2010 to 2023, China-ASEAN trade volume showed an overall growth trend, with bilateral trade volume increasing from US $ 292.8 billion to US $ 911.7 billion, with an average annual growth rate of 11.54%. China and ASEAN will not change their position as each other's largest trading partner for a period of time.

Table 8 China-ASEAN trade volume, growth rate and its proportion in China's foreign trade from 2010 to 2023

Year	China-ASEAN trade volume (Billions of dollars)	Speed increase (%)	China-ASEAN trade accounts for the proportion of China's trade (%)
2010	2928	37.5	9.85
2011	3628.5	24	9.96
2012	4000.9	10.2	10.35
2013	4436	10.9	10.67
2014	4804	8.3	11.17
2015	4721.6	-1.7	11.94
2016	4522	-4.2	12.27
2017	5148	13.8	12.53
2018	5878.7	14.1	12.72
2019	6414.6	9.2	14.01
2020	6846	6.7	14.70
2021	8782	28.1	14.65
2022	9753.4	11.2	15.56
2023	9117	-6.5	15.36

Source: collated according to UN Comtrade and National Bureau of Statistics of China.

3.4.5 Expert perspective: the breakthrough direction of CAFTA 3.0

First, we will continue to improve trade and investment. CAFTA 3.0 is expected to achieve more zero - tariff goods while simplifying customs clearance procedures and strengthening the construction of unified standards, reducing non - tariff barriers and improving trade facilitation through the establishment of unified commodity inspection standards. In the field of service trade, we will accelerate the optimization and upgrading of the supply-side structure of service trade led by digital trade, explore the establishment of a new mode of more efficient service trade management, and improve the risk prevention and control system for the opening up of the service industry. In the field of investment, we should further optimize the regional investment structure and upgrade the industrial layout, promote direct investment in high-tech and high value-added industries, and send positive signals to the international community to enhance the confidence of foreign enterprises in the China-ASEAN market.

Second, we will strengthen cooperation in the digital economy. Through cooperation in the CAFTA version 3.0, we will raise the digital level of countries in the area, narrow the digital divide in the region, and promote member states to share the fruits. First of all, China and ASEAN have reached an agreement and signed a cooperation agreement in the field of digital economy development, giving full play to the driving force of policy highland. On the basis of strengthening cooperation in digital economy infrastructure, China and ASEAN will narrow the gap in digital economy by accelerating technological exchanges and knowledge sharing, building a more efficient, transparent and intelligent supply chain, and accelerating the training of digital talents. To lay a good foundation for cooperation.

Third, we need to accelerate green and sustainable development. The construction of the CAFTA 3.0 is not only a deepening and expansion of previous cooperation achievements, but also an important part of the two sides' joint response to the challenge of global climate change and the promotion of green and low - carbon transformation. With the in - depth development of green economy cooperation between the two sides, the opportunities of green industry continue to expand, the development space continues to increase, and a broader and deeper green economy market will be built. China and ASEAN will continue to strengthen policy coordination and regulatory integration, jointly formulate standards for green economy cooperation, promote the effectiveness of cross - border environmental management and the sustainability of resource utilization, and contribute to the global green economy governance system.

Fourth, we will promote the construction of smart cities to stimulate economic potential. The cooperation between China and ASEAN has also stimulated the economic potential of cities and enhanced their competitiveness. Cities should grasp this opportunity tostrengthen the construction of smart cities, improve governance capacity and service level, start from urban infrastructure construction and public services, accelerate the deep integration of digital economy and urban development, break geographical restrictions and promote resource sharing to achieve sustainable development.

Fifth, we should promote the expansion of 10+1+1 and raise overall welfare. We should speed up the entry into force of the RCEP within ASEAN, reach consensus on the launch of negotiations on Version 3.0 of the CAFTA, and start the construction in accordance with the established procedures. The CAFTA 3.0 can enhance the trade expansion effect, trade diversion effect and trade creation effect of the free trade area, and increase the overall welfare level of China and ASEAN.

Sixth, we will accelerate regional economic cooperation and improve regional integration. On the basis of hardware connectivity, China and ASEAN are also focusing on strengthening soft connectivity such as institutional and regulatory alignment and people‑to‑people exchanges so as to enhance mutual trust and cooperation. In addition, China and ASEAN can make use of their unique advantages to form a strong cooperative and complementary effect, improve international market competitiveness by integrating superior resources, and jointly find and develop potential third‑party markets.